friends OR ENEMIES?

Illustrations copyright © 1997 Guy Parker-Rees

Design by Maria D'Orsi at Wilson Design Associates

Published by Hodder Children's Books 1997

10 9 8 7 6 5 4 3 2 1

ISBN 0 340 68743 6

Printed by Cox and Wyman Ltd, Reading, Berkshire

Hodder Children's Books
A division of Hodder Headline plc
338 Euston Road
London NW1 3BH

friends OR ENEMIES?

by ANITA NAIK

Illustrations by
Guy Parker-Rees

Hodder
Children's
Books

contents

all about Anita

Anita Naik never imagined that she would land her dream job of writing for *Just Seventeen* magazine, but now finds herself the magazine's hugely popular agony aunt, advising thousands of teenage girls on their problems. Anita regularly writes features for loads of other magazines, and is studying counselling and psychotherapy.

On rare days off, Anita sits in cafés people-watching and talking, talking and talking. In fact, it was in various cafés all over the country where Anita did most of her interviews for this book, *Friends or Enemies?* (What a life, huh?) Anita's other books are *Coping with Crushes, Single Again, The Just Seventeen Quiz Book, Am I Normal?, Is this Love?, The Teenage Health Book, Families: can't live with them, can't live without them* and *Respect Yourself*.

Anita was born in London and so far no one – not even her best friend – has been successful in getting her to move.

introduction

Friends can drive you crazy, make you laugh till you cry, lift you up when you're down, shout at you when you're being truly rotten and then forgive you when you shape up. But best of all, friends make the world a nicer place to live in. Good friends will travel miles to talk to you and will move mountains to help you. Yep, friends are worth their weight in gold (or at least CD vouchers).

When I was young all my friends were very much alike. We were all the same age, the same sex, came from similar family backgrounds, and we all lived within shouting distance of one another. Now, I've widened my friendship horizons, and my mates come in all shapes, sizes and colours; are both male and female (and some who are still deciding); and range from 19 to 99 years old. Some still live around the corner, but many of them live hundreds or even thousands of miles away. But have any of these changed how I feel about my friends? No, not one iota. A friend is a friend no matter who they are or where they live.

I can't remember how these friendships were formed, nor can I recall the exact moment when these strangers became friends. All I know is that my friendships are a two-way thing – I will do anything I can for my friends, and I know that my friends will do all they can for me without a second's hesitation.

If you're not sure who your friends are, think about these crucial friendship-revealing situations. Who do you allow to see you when you're having a bad hair/skin/body/mood day? Who's seen you at your very, very worst and survived the ordeal? Who would you tell if you got a date with the guy of your dreams? Whose Lycra shirts do you cry into when your dream date turns into the date from hell? Your best friends' Lycra

shirts, of course. Good friends are the ones who stick by you through thick and thin, through good times and bad. Those who don't, aren't your friends. Simple, agree?

Sure it's possible to survive without any friends. There are lots of occasions when any one of us might have been tempted to think that this friendship lark is just not worth the hassle. But don't be tempted.

Good friends are a godsend. They love you when you're miserable, and they delight in your happiness. They don't judge you on your I.Q., your waist measurement or your bank balance. They like you just for being you. What more could you ask for? Nothing!

CHAPTER one

Finding and making friends

"I am so confused by the whole friendship thing. I don't know if a friendship just happens, or if you can make someone be your friend. If you can make someone your friend, how on earth do you do it?"
Lisa, 14

Having friends is an ace idea, but where do you find them? How do you pick the friends from the fiends? Sadly, it's not always easy. Spotting someone who might make a good buddy is not as simple as going ga-ga, drool, drool over a prospective boyfriend. There are no telltale thumps of the heart, no sweaty palms and absolutely no sensation of falling head-over-heels in love. No, spotting a friend is altogether a more subtle experience. And boy, did I find this out the hard way when my best friend started out as my worst nightmare.

Vici and I had been introduced a number of times, and I thought that I had sent out friendly-type vibes. I was certainly trying to be friendly, but whenever we saw each other at school or passed on the High Street she would ignore me. This cold-shoulder treatment was not on, said I, so I retaliated by telling everyone that she was a nose-in-the-air snob. That'll teach her I thought. She, in turn, told everyone that I was a mean and pathetic low-life. For months and months this battle raged. Me saying one

thing, and she dreaming up some other bit of girlie abuse. To say that our relationship started out on the wrong foot is a bit of a rash understatement. Then one day I literally bumped into Vici at the opticians. After I had picked myself up off the floor I found out that her cold-shoulder behaviour had more to do with myopia than snootiness. She wasn't being rude, she just couldn't see me. Talk about misjudging someone! She's now been one of my closest friends for over ten years, and we still laugh about how our relationship started as hate at first sight.

The only way to work out who will make a good friend is to take a risk. If someone makes a friendly overture to you, then return the gesture and see what happens. It may work out, it may not.

Friend-finding mission

So, where will you find some friends? Well, it's no good sitting in your bedroom trying to wish them out of thin air. They simply won't materialise. The only way to make friendships happen is to be pro-active. In other words, you have to get off your butt. You have to get out there among the human race, find some people that you might like and then get with the mingling. Then once you're in mingling mode you have to make your move – you have to show that you're a friendly bod. All your mingling will be for nought if you leave your friendly face at home in a jar.

The other thing that you have to do when on a friend-finding mission is to keep an open mind. Don't be too judgemental or let previous bad experiences with friends affect your attitude or choice. Anyone and everyone can be a friend if you let them.

Where to look

" I don't really have any proper friends. I would desperately like to make some, but I don't know where to go or what to do. It's not as if you can go to a shop and order some."
Tina, 15

Tina's right, making friends is not like ordering a pizza or buying a pair of shoes. This is a bit of a pity because it would be so easy just to pop into the Friends-4-U shop and buy an ice-skating buddy, a homework partner, a trusted confidante, and a friend with a huge wardrobe. But as Friends-4-U doesn't exist, the whole business of finding friends is left to us. But, fear not, because while some friends are found in the most unlikely places (the opticians, for example), most are right under our collective noses. In others words, you don't have to go very far to find them.

Good places to start searching are those where you'll find peeps that are into the stuff you're into. You might not necessarily find a friend at one of these places, but at least you won't bore each other stupid during the process of finding out.

LOCAL VOLUNTARY GROUPS – You and a prospective friend already share a common interest so it will be easy to start a conversation. And because these groups meet regularly there will be lots of opportunities for friendship to grow. So while you're out doing some good for the community, you can also be doing yourself a bit of good.

AFTER-SCHOOL GROUPS – Throw your enthusiasm into one of these and you can combine a fascinating pursuit with making a new friend. If your school doesn't run an after-school group that holds any interest for you, why not set one up?

SPORTS CLUBS – Many strong friendships have developed because of a shared passion for a particular sport. I've heard that there's nothing better for breaking the ice than ice-skating.

"One of my friends is a girl I met on a bus in Italy years ago. Even though she lives in Canada, she is a good pal. We write long letters to each other and share all our deepest thoughts. It doesn't matter that we can't go to the flicks together because I know she's a special friend. She can make me laugh without saying a word."
Annie, 15

PEN PALS – Even if you live in the middle of nowhere, a pen pal is someone you can confide in. Some pen pal relationships become so strong that the letter writers just have to meet each other face-to-face.

FRIENDS OF FRIENDS – If a friend introduced you to one of their friends, and they introduced you to another of their friends and so on, imagine how many mates you'd end up with! Now, that's what I call a party.

HOLIDAY CLUBS – These places are great for making friends. For a start, it's unlikely that many of the kids will know each other and therefore all of you will be looking to find a reassuring buddy to hang out with. Secondly, holiday clubs go to great lengths to create an atmosphere in which friendships can blossom. Ahhhh!

WEEKEND CRAFT OR ACTIVITY CLASSES – In these classes you will find peeps with similar passions. If you're into acting, then a Saturday theatre group is where you'll most probably find a soulmate. Want to learn pottery and make a friend? Then join a pottery class, and while you're making a slab pot look around for a friendly face.

SIBLINGS – Oh no, you cry, there is no way in the world that I could make a friend out of my brother and sister. Why not, I ask. Nothing in common? Doubt it. Your brother or sister live too far away? Not likely.

They don't like you? Now that's a distinct possibility, but appearances can be deceiving. No, there's really no good excuse for not having a sibling as a friend.

A brother or sister could be the best friend you'll ever have. It won't mean that you won't fight over the hair–dryer or whose turn it is to do the washing-up, but you can still be friends. And let's face it, an ally at home has got to be worth ten at school. Think about it.

RIGHT UNDER YOUR NOSE – Some people are friends, but you just haven't realised it. You've been rubbing shoulders with someone for so long that you've taken for granted the trust that's developed between you. So have a quick peep to see if a friend is lurking nearby.

"I'm the only teenage girl in my small village and I didn't have any girl friends that I could hang around with after school or on weekends. When I realised that a friend doesn't have to mean a girl friend, I made the effort to be friendly towards two local boys. At first they didn't want anything to do with me, but I kept trying and now we get on brilliantly."
Katie, 14

"Rosie was a friend of my grandmother's. When my gran died I used to go and visit Rosie all the time. Over the years we have become real friends. She's not like my friends at school, but I can still tell her everything. I trust her opinion and always go to her when I have a tough problem."
Kate, 17

Both Katie and Kate found friendship where they least expected to find it. Their experiences show that friendship has nothing to do with age or sex, but everything to do with forming happy bonds with someone else.

Making friends

So you've found a person that you'd like to be friends with. She (or he!) is good company, funny, and also seems to be interested in making a friend. What next? Well, if you're a confident and easy-to-talk-to type of gal, you can miss this section. If not, then you might want a little help.

How to make friends when you're shy

"I don't have many friends because I'm shy. I never know what to say, so I say nothing. Why can't I be funny and clever like all the other girls?"
Sue, 14

Shyness is probably the biggest hurdle to making friends. It stops you talking to people, returning friendly smiles and can even stop you from leaving your bedroom. If you're so shy that you find it nigh impossible to talk to anyone, then it's time you realised the following:

1 Everyone suffers from bouts of shyness, and everyone (no matter how confident and outgoing they may appear to be) worries that other people aren't going to like them.

2 No one is judging you or waiting for you to do something embarrassing. Believe me, people are far too busy worrying about themselves to care what you're up to.

3 If you don't make the effort to show people that you are friendly, then they won't make the effort with you. You have to deck the urge to go hide behind a large piece of furniture and ignore the fact that your stomach is doing somersaults, your knees are knocking together and your heart is racing. (I know all about this stuff – I've been through it myself.)

4 Don't keep stalling by saying that you will try to be more outgoing next time. There is never going to be a better time than now for making friends, so hop to it!

So the first thing you've got to do to kill shyness and woo people is SMILE! Get in some smiling practice by going to your front gate (now!) and smiling warmly at the postman, the meter reader and folks walking their dogs. I have no doubt that all these people will give you a cheesy in return. See, you're on to a winner when you smile.

Now that you've got their attention, say HELLO! Follow up this ice-breaker with a bit of everyday-type chit-chat.

The secret of making conversation is to ask questions. Everyone likes to talk about themselves or to express their opinions. All you've got to do is listen and look interested. If you don't listen you won't know what to say when the conversation moves back to you. If you look interested in what they're saying, they'll be flattered. And as we all know, flattery will get you everywhere.

If all this goes all wrong (but it's not likely), then there's no shame in actually admitting that you're a tad shy and that you find it hard to talk to people. At least folks will know that it's shyness, not unfriendliness, that makes you appear so reserved.

That's all you have to do to give shyness its marching orders: crack a cheesy and say Hello! Dead simple.

How to make friends when you're new to an area

"We moved here two months ago and I hate it. I had to leave my friends and my boyfriend behind. All the girls in my new school have already made friends, so I'm always on my own."
Shannon, 15

Moving to a new area is tough. It usually means leaving all your old friends behind, fitting into a new school where everyone is already paired-off, and having to act happy about the situation for the sake of your parents. The first thing you've got to do is let go of the past. This doesn't mean dumping your old mates and forgetting about the good times. It means accepting that you're somewhere new and that you can't go back to how it was. Holding on to the past is a barrier against moving on. Sure, things will never be the same again, but this doesn't mean that things won't be just as good or even better.

Next thing to do is ask your classmates about good places to hang out, or which school groups are worth joining. When you've got the conversation going, ask some of the girls round to your house. Don't rush it, just take it slowly so that your would-be mates realise that you're just being friendly and not trying to muscle in on their existing friendships.

By the way, had you realised (or were you too busy being sullen and depressed) that as the new kid on the block, everyone wants to know all about you? All you have to do is SMILE to knock down the barriers.

How to make friends when you have a reputation

"Everyone thinks I'm a slag because I got off with someone else's boyfriend two years ago. It was a mistake, but no one will give me a second chance. If I do manage to make a new friend, I know she'll dump me when she hears the story."
Dawn, 15

Having a 'reputation' can be off-putting to prospective friends. Whether the reputation is warranted or not, the important thing to remember is that it's not up to others to pass judgement on you. We all make mistakes and we all pay for them. If so-called friends keep raking up your past, or tell you that they can't be pals because of it, then make the break there and then and don't even bother to defend yourself.

A good way to knock this problem on the head is to be honest and open about your past. Mention it to your new friend early in the relationship. This will be your chance to say your piece before someone tries to put a spanner in the works. Your friend's reaction will also let you know just what sort of a friend she is going to be. Is she going to be the type who'll sell you down the river, or will she prove to be a truly supportive pal?

If you're always in trouble with the police and your school, or you are a bully, then you can't expect people to welcome your friendship with open arms. To rectify this situation you'll need to do more than smile. You're going to have to change your behaviour.

How to make friends when you're worried about your image

"I really like Tina, but she's so square. Everyone makes fun of her because she's a computer nerd. She makes no effort with her appearance and sometimes she doesn't even bother to brush her hair. We could be mates if only she'd shape up."
Christine, 16

We're all destined to meet people who don't fit into our vision of the perfect friend. They might be younger or older than yourself, they may not be cool enough, or they may come from a very different background to your own. But in spite of, or even because of these differences, you want to be friends.

If you let superficial things (or even superficial friends) dictate who you can and can't be friends with, you're limiting the depth and the extent of your friendships. Friends who are different serve a dual purpose: they let you broaden your horizons and also make you challenge your prejudices.

It's not easy to stand up to the heckling of your peers and be friends with someone who refuses to go with the crowd. It might mean that you'll be an outsider for a while or will lose some of your more shallow and ignorant friends. However, if you're only going to pick friends who look good, say the right things, go to the in places and wear right-on clothes, it doesn't say much about your character.

The key to having successful friendships is in having a relationship that lets both partners be themselves. Try it, you might even find it fun!

How to make friends when you're different

"Just because I wear hippy-like clothes, talk about
animal rights and live a different kind of life to the other girls
in my class, no one wants to be friends with me. They say that
my parents are weirdos because they travel around the country
campaigning for the environment. I hate myself the way I am.
I desperately wish I could be like the other girls."
Ellie, 15

Most people go through their school years wishing they were like everyone else. They think that everyone else is normal, well-adjusted and happy, and that they are the lone oddball. They think that everyone else skates through life on greased blades without a hair out of place or a zit in sight. Rubbish! The truth is everyone feels, thinks, behaves and looks different – there is no 'everyone else'. And there are certainly no zitless teenagers in my neck of the woods – there are only people who are better at hiding their differences (and their zits).

Unfortunately, these pretenders make up the bulk of the population, and they make it hard for those who aren't so good at concealing their true personalities. If you're feeling alienated because you 'don't fit in', don't be ashamed. But more importantly, don't try to change yourself so that you fit in with the crowd.

If you think that your 'differences' are stopping you from making friends, you could be misreading the whole situation. It isn't being different that stops friendships, it's low self-image. So if you start to feel good about yourself and proud of your individuality, then you'll like yourself more and so will others.

As for thinking that no one wants to be friends with you, just take a closer look. Sure, the in-clique may keep their distance, but so what? Who really wants to be friends with bods who can only think in a crowd? Believe me, if you took the time to look over the up-turned noses of the clique there's bound to be some intelligent souls who just can't wait to make your acquaintance.

How friendships grow

Friendships aren't instantaneous things, they take time to develop. Some friendships grow quite quickly over a matter of weeks or months, while others take years and years. Sadly, some friendships don't last the

distance and fizzle out before a meaningful bond has had time to be established. But however long a friendship is in the making it will go through certain stages. See if you can recognise these stages in your current friendships.

1 You meet someone and decide that you like them. Good news is, they seem to like you as well.

2 You begin to trust them and therefore start to share the ups and downs of your life. You are also happy to listen to your friend's problems.

3 You look forward to seeing or speaking to them and having a good time. And each time you get together, each of you opens up a little more.

4 You start to include them in your plans and look to them for advice and help. You realise that your friend is doing likewise. The two of you have built up a strong relationship based on mutual trust and respect.

A beautiful thing has happened – a friendship has been born.

The secret of making friends

BE PATIENT AND SENSITIVE
No matter how much you like someone, don't demand too much, too soon; it may freak the other person out. No one likes to be pushed into things, nor to feel suffocated by another's attentions. Chill out, and let the relationship grow naturally.

LISTEN TO YOUR OWN CONSCIENCE
If a prospective friend does something that makes you feel uncomfortable, don't be afraid to back off. Likewise, if someone makes you feel bad about yourself, then dump them – they're no good for you. So that bad feelings aren't left to ferment and therefore cloud whatever remains of the friendship, be up front and let them know what's bugging you.

LEARN TO BE TRUSTING
It's impossible to have a friendship if there is no element of trust. Both partners have to be open, honest and not afraid to say no.

BE FORGIVING
Some people just can't cut it in the friendship stakes; they may let you down, stand you up, or blab something that was meant to be just between the two of you. What you've got to do is understand the limits of particular friendships.

You must not think that one disappointing friendship means that they'll all be disappointing. Learn to understand and forgive your friends their shortcomings. There will be some people who will always be there for you, and there will be others who won't.

IT'S OKAY TO HAVE LOTS OF FRIENDS
Without being at all disloyal, you can have different friends for different things. Some mates are ice-skating buddies, others are school pals and others you only see once a week at dance class. To some friends you will be an open book and they will know all your deepest, darkest fears. Other friends will only know the barest details. That's fine. Don't get worked up about making every friend a best friend.

CHAPTER **two**

What is a good friend?

To discover what you want from your friendships, write down five qualities that you expect to find in your friends. Your list might include some of the following: a sense of humour, loyalty, self-respect, generosity, honesty, reliability, tolerance, compassion and integrity. You might like to include in your list hobbies or passions that you would like your friends to share. For example, if you're really into sport then you might expect that your best buddies would also like getting hot and sweaty in the gym or on the pitch.

Ask a few chums to also make one of these lists and then get together to

compare notes. You'll probably find that two or three items will appear on everyone's list. It is these things that make you all mates.

But don't worry if your list and that of a good friend don't overlap. For example, it's not dead crucial if your friend prefers to couch-out while you do a mini-marathon. What's really important is that she understands how much you like athletics and is enthusiastically tolerant of your commitment. Likewise, you should be tolerant of her commitment to couch potato-dom. Sometimes the strongest friendships are between people who are like chalk and cheese – totally opposite.

"Carla and I are best mates but we're also very different. She's hip, clubby and trendy, I'm not. I'm into swimming, she's not. Our friends can't understand why we get on so well. I know that Carla's club friends think I'm boring, but we don't care. We know that our friendship can survive anything."
Tina, 15

The fundamentals of being a good friend

LOYALTY – To be loyal means that your friends can rely on you, and you on them, through thick and thin.

We all know what good-time pals are. They're the ones who only want to be with you when you're happy and things are going smoothly. They hang around for the laughs but rack off when times are tough. But how about bad-time pals? Did you know that there are some people who positively delight in someone else's misery? This is sad, but true. These people like being involved in the dramatic to-ing and fro-ing of dying romances, they like to be around when teachers are giving you grief, and they dine out on your personal problems. But do these bods help? Do they make any attempt to make things better? No way! In fact, they go out of their way to stir up more trouble, turning a crisis into a disaster just so that the drama remains at fever pitch. And when the drama's over and everyone is more or less happy, they quickly move on to find another trouble spot.

Do these sad souls know the meaning of the word 'loyalty'? No. Do

24

they have any of the qualities of a good friend? No. These guys give lessons to Cruella de Vil on the finer points of being nasty.

"I had two friends who were brilliant when my boyfriend left me. They came to see me every day and they would let me talk endlessly about how I felt. They agreed with every nasty thought I had about him and boys in general. But when I started to feel better, these supposed friends turned real nasty. They threw cold water on my suggestion that I might start going out again. They said I was idiotic to even contemplate finding a new boyfriend. Anyway, I did find a new boyfriend and you know what these two 'chums' did? They said he looked like the two-timing kind. I finally realised that they were only interested in me being miserable."
Janey, 17

Loyal friends don't tell someone how to live their life; they are supportive without being judgemental, and caring without any hint of self-interest. Loyalty also goes hand-in-hand with honesty. Good mates will say something if they feel that a friend is heading into trouble. Read Karen's letter to see what being supportive and honest is all about.

"My sister is my best friend because she's always stuck by me. A few years back I was anorexic and my school friends tried to pretend that nothing was wrong. It was my sister who talked to me about it and phoned up the clinic. At first I accused her of being disloyal, but if it wasn't for her loyalty and honesty I might be dead now. I can't thank my sister enough."
Karen, 16

LETTING FRIENDS BE THEMSELVES – It isn't easy to let your friends do things that don't involve you. Suddenly you feel unimportant and sort of unnecessary. You worry that your friends will drop you when they find someone else who is into the things they are into. This is a very natural fear. No one likes the thought that they may lose their friends.

"Steph is really into music and has started hanging out at this club. She invites me to come along but I don't like the club scene. I hate the way she's changed. I want the old Steph and our old friendship back. "

Lara, 15

It's important to accept that everybody changes and that change is not a bad thing. In most cases it's a positive sign that your friends are growing as people. And if your friends are happy with their new interests, then you as a good friend should also be happy.

Imagine how you would feel if your friends knocked the fact that you had discovered a talent for dancing and were doing all they could to rain on your parade. You might assume they were miserable souls who were stuck in a rut, jealous or terribly insecure. If anything could test your friendships, this would.

If friends attempt to control the lives of their mates for purely selfish reasons, then the relationships are in deep trouble. But if friends go with the flow and try to show some enthusiasm for their friends' new interests, the relationships will be happy and healthy ones.

Fiona found out all about her own selfish motives when her best friend, Jessie, joined the school computer club.

"Jessie has always been good with computers but when she joined the computer club I found it really hard to take. All she would talk about was computers and web sites – stuff that I know nothing about. Frankly, she was becoming a bore and a bit of an embarrassment. All the nerdy kids are in the computer club and I didn't want her to become one of them. I didn't want my friend to be seen as a nerd, and I didn't want to be seen hanging around with a nerd. I begged her to leave the club but she went berserk. She said that if I didn't like her the way she was, then I wasn't a real friend. She told me that she didn't want to see me any more. I got such a fright but it made me realise just how selfish I had been."

Fiona, 15

If you don't allow your friends to be themselves it is a reflection of your own insecurity. If you're finding it tough letting your mates develop their own interests then be honest about it. Tell your friends why it bothers you, and if they are good friends they will reassure you that whatever happens you're still the best of pals. See, honesty pays.

Take note: friends don't have to agree on everything, spend every minute in each other's company, nor do they have to be clones of one another. Friends are simply people who like being with each other, despite any differences.

LEARNING TO FORGIVE AND FORGET – Arguments, fights and disagreements are a part of all relationships, even good ones. If you're lucky your friendships will suffer only a few bad scenes. But on the whole, arguments and heated discussions are pretty healthy ways of self-expression. They let you air your grievances, get annoying things off your chest and they also give relationships a chance to develop. You never know what you and your friends might discover about yourselves and each other after a ripping argument. The important thing about having a good old argy-bargy is forgiving and forgetting. Lou found out about this the hard way.

"The biggest argument I had with my friend Jill started over something really silly. She forgot to pick up something for me when she was on the way to my house. I went ballistic. As far as I was concerned her selfish stupidity and unreliability was the last straw. I yelled at her like I have never yelled at anyone before. Jill, of course, didn't talk to me for days. Our friendship could have been ruined if Jill hadn't finally come around to see me. She said that I was right about her being unreliable and she promised that she would try to change. I apologised for being such a witch and, thank goodness, she forgave me."
Lou, 15

Making relationships work requires flexibility and a lot of give and take. No one is perfect, so no one can expect perfection in their friends.

Sometimes you will do the wrong thing and jeopardise a friendship; sometimes your friends will do something rotten. What can be relied on though is that good friends who have a sound relationship can forgive and forget.

"Sue is my best friend but she used to be so irritating and annoying. She did things like turn up half an hour late and then take another half an hour to get ready. She wouldn't apologise for her behaviour, but became really stroppy if I got mad with her. One day she asked what she'd done to annoy me and I just said 'Nothing', but then suddenly I just let it all pour out. Sue was really calm and said 'Oh, why didn't you say something before?' I almost ruined our friendship for the sake of a few words and little bit of honesty."
Paula, 16

Sadly there are times when forgiving and forgetting are not enough. Sometimes a friendship has been stretched to its limits and there's no way it can be saved. This can happen when friends discover that someone has been hurtfully disloyal. There is a line that has to be drawn – some things are worth getting over and some things aren't.

"Chris and I have been friends since we were seven years old. I regarded her as my best friend, even though she was always flirting with my boyfriends. One time I pulled her up on it and she apologised saying that it would never happen again, but it did. When she actually stole my boyfriend from me, I broke off our friendship. Chris apologised and wouldn't stop crying but it was too late – I no longer trusted her. I wasn't even sure if I liked her. There are some things you just can't forgive."
Liz, 17

COMMUNICATING – This may seem dead obvious but you'd be surprised at how often relationships are blown because the partners don't talk honestly and candidly to each other. If you're irritated with a friend or

feel hurt by something she has done then you shouldn't be afraid to say so. After all, if friends can't communicate, then what kind of friendship do you have?

If you can't be open with your friends, it is because you don't trust them. Perhaps you feel that your friends can't give you what you need. The most common reason for not being open with people is the fear that they will be angry with you. If any of these sound familiar then it really is time to talk. Like the man says, it's good to talk!

"I fell out with one of my friends because I forgot her birthday. For a whole year she went out of her way to avoid me. Naturally I thought she'd gone off me, so I avoided her as well. It got to the stage where we wouldn't even look at each other. Then one day she sent me a letter asking why I hated her. I was totally shocked and told her that I thought she hated me

for missing her birthday. We both realised that we had been fools. Thankfully we sorted it all out and our friendship is now stronger than ever."
Marie, 15

BEING SUPPORTIVE – This means caring enough about your friendship to do something, even when you're afraid of the consequences. When you put yourself in the firing-line in order to help someone, it shows that you are a true friend who is thinking more about others than about herself. It's not easy to step in, say your piece and offer to help a friend when others are hiding their heads in the sand.

"I realised Charlotte was a true friend when my father walked out with his secretary. I was so embarrassed and hurt by what he'd done that I pretended that it hadn't happened. All of my friends knew about it but no one would say anything. Even the neighbours looked the other way when they saw me. But Charlotte was different – she came right up to me and said that she was sorry to hear about my father and asked how I was feeling. It was such a relief to stop pretending and to know that someone cared."
Dinah, 16

Take note: good friends also know when not to get involved.

How to keep a good thing going

You've got finding and making friends sussed. You also know all about what it takes to be a good friend. Now it's time to work out the dos and don'ts of keeping the flames of a new friendship raging. Let's start off with the things you don't do.

DON'T:

- dump new friends when old friends reappear on the scene
- ditch new friends when the love of your life pops around
- tell everyone your friends' secrets

- take your friends for granted
- let your friends down at the last minute
- bully your friends into doing what you want
- refuse to listen to what they have to say

THINGS TO DO:

PLAN STUFF – Take the initiative to plan outings with your new buddies. This lets new friends know that you want to see them and be with them. Don't be backward in coming forward, and forget all about any fears of rejection – just blast on in there with some ideas for having fun, fun, fun!

IF YOU'RE TICKED OFF, SHARE IT – Nice people don't get mad – rubbish! A good friendship means being able to say that you're ticked off plenty. If you keep it to yourself, your anger will fester away and eat at your friendships. But when you do say something, say it calmly and show that once the air is cleared you can forget all about it. If your friends apologise, accept their apology gracefully and don't keep banging on about it.

DO UNTO OTHERS – How many times have you done something to a friend that, if the tables were turned, would send you into a raging fury?

Once? Twice? Heaps? You know the sorts of situations I'm talking about: keeping your options open for a night out just in case a better offer comes along; pushing your friends to one side when a boyfriend appears; or for the sake of keeping face with another set of friends, you slag off your other friends. Such despicable behaviour has only one outcome – you end up alone and friendless.

If you want to keep your new friends, then 'Do unto others as you would have them do unto you'. Enough said?

MAKE TIME – Friendships need time to develop. Simply going out together four Fridays in a row does not a friendship maketh. Nor do minute-long chit-chats in the corridor between science and French maketh for a meaningful relationship. Good friendships grow slowly, so be patient, understanding and willing to put in the necessary effort.

The roles we play

I used to believe that in order to be friends with people you had to think and act the same as them. This meant never disagreeing and never ever admitting that you liked or believed in different things. In short, I tried to live up to my friends' every expectation. I did nothing out of the ordinary, I said only what I knew would be acceptable and I certainly kept quiet about any special aspirations I had. Keeping up this front was hard work. And you know why I was like this? Because I didn't want to disappoint them by showing them who I really was. Was I a girl with a self-esteem problem? You bet! Thankfully, I've seen the light and realise that you can disagree with someone, be yourself and still be friends.

However, in trying to be a 'good friend' we can get trapped in certain roles and find that we can't escape them. Sometimes these traps are of our own making, in other words we make ourselves out to be someone we're not. At other times we get hopelessly caught up in everyone else's idea of who we are. Following are three of the most common roles that can ensnare each and every one of us.

THE JOKER – We all know someone who can be relied upon for a good laugh. They are the life and soul of a party and the first one to do

something wild or totally outrageous. Everyone loves The Joker because they make life fun. The downside is that their friends are often reluctant to let them be anything other than the comedian.

"Whenever I'm in the dumps my friends say, 'Don't be like that. You're meant to be the happy one'. What they don't know is that I often get depressed and need a shoulder to cry on. I don't want to be funny all the time! I hate what my friends make me do – I feel that no one really knows me."
Gayle, 15

"I'm known for doing crazy things, like dancing on tables in McDonalds, kissing boys in the street and playing practical jokes. Everyone thinks I'm wacky, but it's all a lie. I'm afraid my friends won't like me if they know the real me. The me who is shy and quiet."

Yas, 15

If you can see a way out of the role-play that's fine, but there are many who convince themselves that if all this pretending is good for their friends, then it must good for them as well. This is so wrong. It is also dishonest. The Joker is showing that she doesn't trust her friends to like the real person, and by always wearing a happy face she is cheating herself of healthy emotions. A true friend is truthful about who she is and what she feels.

What The Joker has to do:

1 Let her friends see the real person no matter how uncomfortable and embarrassing it may feel at first.

2 Not be the life and soul of the party all the time. She should rage when she wants to rage, and be quiet when she wants to be quiet.

3 Ask her friends why it isn't okay for her to be sad, and why it is that they don't take her feelings seriously.

4 Not hide her true feelings behind a cloak of humour.

THE PROBLEM SOLVER – I get lots of letters at *Just Seventeen* from girls complaining that everyone treats them like an agony aunt. And speaking as an agony aunt I know where they're coming from.

It's tough when you're seen as everyone's problem solver. Sometimes it seems that you alone have the right answers, that you alone have the only shoulder to cry on, and that you're the only one in the whole world with a full box of tissues. Friends forget that you too have problems that need to be talked out.

AGONY AUNT

People take on roles because they want to hide something about themselves. Just as The Joker may be secretly shy, The Problem Solver often gets involved with other people's problems to avoid looking at her own. If you think this is what you are doing, you have to put a 'Closed' sign on your bedroom door and direct your home-spun wisdom into your own life. To see the problem from both sides, read Sue's and Jenny's letters.

"The thing that bugs me is that no one cares when I have a problem. They think I'm okay because I can solve their problems, so they don't bother to support me. Not even Jenny my best friend seems to understand."
Sue, 14

"I never knew Sue felt the way she does. In all the time I've known her I never heard her tell someone something personal about herself. She gives the impression that she is totally together and doesn't need anyone's help, especially mine".
Jenny, 14

What The Problem Solver has to do:

1 Drop the guilts. It's possible to be a good friend without having to listen to everyone's tales of woe.

2 She should give advice if she thinks she has something valuable to offer, but otherwise she should take a step back and let her friends sort out their own problems.

3 Stop her friends from involving her in their personal problems.

4 When she has a problem, she must ask for help. If this means showing her friends that she's human and not infallible, then so be it.

THE LOSER – Within a group of friends there is usually someone who is always on the receiving end of jokes and teasing; someone who always seems to slip on the banana skin, fall in the mud or be simply unlucky. If you're this someone, then it's time to give yourself a break.

Teasing, while often meant in harmless fun can cross the line and becoming a form of bullying. Another problem with being seen as The Loser is that the role can become a self-fulfilling prophecy. After all, if your closest friends don't have faith in you, who will?

> *"The teasing started off as a joke because once I had a run of bad luck. Since then it's always me who falls, gets dumped, or gets into trouble. If there's a joke to be made, it's usually made about me. For a while it didn't bother me but now I'm beginning to think that people actually believe that I'm some sort of hapless, hopeless fool. I'm sure people are waiting for me to fail so that they can make a joke out of it. The problem is, I usually live up to their expectations."*
> Kelly, 15

To break this nasty cycle, The Loser has to:

1 Stand up for herself by telling her friends that she's unhappy about the way she is being treated. She deserves respect just like everyone else.

2 Believe that when she is honest with her friends they will still be her friends. If they won't, will she be losing anything of value? I doubt it.

3 Take stock of her achievements. She then has to ask her friends why they never make positive comments about these things.

CHAPTER **three**

Bad friends, bad news

This is not the nicest of subjects but we all have to be wary of making bad friends or forming bad relationships. Bad friends will betray you, let you down, use you and lead you into trouble (for example, drug-taking, getting drunk, shoplifting and generally being a pain to all and sundry). In short, bad-news friends shows you no respect at all, and bad relationships can go nowhere but down.

While it's not hard to speak out when a stranger is mean to you, it's often very difficult to do the same when friends are the cause of the trouble. And because this is so difficult we often take the easy way out and blame ourselves. What we do is say things like: "What did I do wrong? My friends wouldn't do this to me unless I'd hurt them or done something rotten to them in the beginning", "I'm so weak and pathetic it isn't any wonder that my friends are lousy" or "It's not my friends' fault. Bad things just happen to them". Read the following letter to get a real-world example of how easy it is to make excuses for a bad friend.

"Every time Janey did something horrible to me I'd explain it away: I'd annoyed her or it was a joke or I was too sensitive. It took me ages to realise that she was just plain nasty."

Justine, 15

THINGS BAD FRIENDS DO:

- ☛ tell lies
- ☛ turn up late
- ☛ reveal your secrets
- ☛ desert you when you are in trouble
- ☛ dump you when a boy comes on the scene
- ☛ only see you when they want something
- ☛ put you down
- ☛ constantly criticise, tease or bully you
- ☛ never stick up for you
- ☛ gossip about you
- ☛ let you down

What to do about bad friends

The best way to tell if you've got bad friends is to think about how they make you feel. If being with them makes you feel scared, miserable or guilty then it's time to have a really good look at your friendship.

"Being with Liz was really strange. I couldn't put my finger on what she did but I always came home feeling really bad about myself. Then she went away on holiday for a month and I realised how relieved I was that I didn't have to see her. I also realised that she was being nasty to me under the pretence of being a 'friend'. It was a revelation and it enabled me to make the decision to stop seeing her."

Fiona, 17

If you decide, like Fiona did, that you have a bad friend the first thing to do is to decide whether or not you can live with it. For example, I have a friend who is notoriously unpunctual. Over the years I have missed the start of umpteen films and lost count of the number of times I've waited in the rain. On one occasion her lateness made me almost miss a plane! The final straw was the day that she was so late that I thought she'd been in a terrible accident. I was about to call the police, when in she breezed loaded down with shopping bags! Furious with her selfishness, I decided that I would never see her again. I gradually calmed down and we worked out a compromise. I would wait fifteen minutes for her to turn up and if she hadn't appeared, I would leave. The arrangement works fine and even her time-keeping has improved.

Weighing up the pros and cons of a friendship is important. In every friendship there are some things that can be overlooked, other things that can be worked out, and one or two things that need to be stamped out. When the bad outweighs the good, it's time to move on. As the saying goes: With bad friends, who needs enemies.

The five deadly friendship sins

BETRAYAL – Being lied to or betrayed by friends is painful and distressing. Our friends are so important to us that when they betray us, it is like the end of the world. In one fell swoop we've been hurt and lost the only people who would have provided support and reassurance.

"Sarah was my closest friend, I told her everything. I trusted her more than anyone and would have done anything for her. That was until she betrayed me, now I'll never speak to her again. It still hurts to say it, but she had an affair with my boyfriend. I miss him but I miss her more. I don't understand why she risked our friendship for a quick fling. Why didn't she think of my feelings rather than her feelings for my boyfriend? The whole thing has made me very wary of friendships."
Steph, 17

Few betrayals hurt as much as having a girl friend who gets involved with your boyfriend. This low act is so hard to forgive and forget that few friendships survive it. Sue paid a high price when she cheated on her friend Helen:

"I don't know why I did it to Helen. I guess I was jealous of what she had so when her boyfriend made a pass at me I gave in – I never meant it to go so far. I told Helen that I was truly sorry but it was too late. She wouldn't forgive me and I don't blame her. Helen still ignores me, and when I see her with new friends I realise how much I've lost."
Sue, 16

If you're tempted to betray a friend then you need to work out why you're so willing to ruin a friendship. Is it revenge? Jealousy? Is it because you believe that a boyfriend is worth more than a girl friend? Whatever your decision, bear in mind that good friendships are hard to find.

Surviving betrayal

1 Keep clear of the betrayer. This will let you get on with your life without having to confront her every day. This is not 'chickening out', this is about doing what is best for you. If you feel that you have to clear the air, then you must do so very calmly. You never know, once you've talked with your friend you may even be able to start the friendship anew.

2 Don't be afraid to trust people. Betrayers, thankfully, are few and far between. Putting the past behind you and learning to trust someone new is a bit like breaking up with a guy: you grieve, you get angry, you get over him and then you find someone new.

3 Forget any plans you have to take sweet revenge on the betrayer. You can't afford to waste your energy on something so negative.

4 If you meet your ex-friend, don't bring up the past. You have to either forgive her or forget her.

POSSESSIVENESS AND JEALOUSY – These are the big enemies of good friendships. If you have friends who are possessive and jealous, watch out! These two nasty characteristics can cause perfectly nice friends to become perfectly destructive fiends. The only way to deal with such friends is to reassure them. Tell them (if it's the truth) that your liking other people doesn't lessen your friendship with them. At the same time, don't give in to their demands – it will just make matters worse.

"I thought that if I spent more time with Becky she wouldn't be so clingy, but I was wrong. She started to expect me to do more and more things with her. Every time I went off without her she'd act like I'd done something terrible. I'd feel guilty and fall back in with her again."

Danni, 15

How to spot the jealous and possessive ones

1 They won't want you to have other friends. Period.

2 They will become angry or sulk if you go out with anyone else.

3 They will be secretly glad when you break up with your boyfriend.

4 They will be happy when you're down in the dumps and need their emotional support.

5 They will either say negative things about the hobbies that they don't share with you, or will change all their hobbies so that they are the same as yours.

6 They will be totally paranoid if you say you can't go out with them.

7 Their jealousy and insecurity will stop them from congratulating you when you achieve something.

While it's easy to sympathise with someone who is suffering from these things (after all, they're a sign of how bad they feel about themselves), it's important to remember that this sort of friendship is not a balanced and healthy one. For example, if your friends are jealous and possessive, can they be relied upon for honest and candid support or will they always have their own self-interests at heart? The only way to deal with this situation, especially if the friendships are worth saving, is to discuss the problem openly. Tell them that their behaviour and attitude is destroying you and your friendship.

Three's a crowd

While most of us can control our possessiveness and jealousy, there are times when it can sneak up and get the better of us. One of the critical times is when a happy twosome becomes a threesome.

"I hate Vicky because she's trying to take Kim away from me. Kim and I were best friends but now that Vicky's around, everything's different. I feel like telling Vicky to get lost."
Paula, 16

"I didn't mind when Sue started hanging out with Katie and me. We had lots of things in common and we did have some great times. But then things went funny. I wasn't being asked to go out with them as much, and Sue and Katie started to share all these in-jokes that I didn't understand. Now they act like I'm the one intruding on their friendship."
Anna, 15

Thing is, this whole twosome/threesome thing can be avoided really easily. All that you and your friends have got to understand is that people can have lots of really good friends. And having lots of friends does not imply that you are disloyal, fickle or a bit of a control freak.

"Sara and I have been good friends since we were seven. We've always hung out together and been cool with each other. Then last year she became friends with this new girl in her school, Sian. I liked Sian but Sara didn't seem to want Sian and me to be friends. She would set us up against each other and then take sides. One minute I was the favourite, the next Sian was. I hated what she was doing but I didn't know how to deal with it. Now Sian and I hate each other. Though Sara complains about it, I think she secretly likes this animosity because it means she can keep me all to herself."
Laura, 16

Instead of fighting it out, Sian and Laura would have been better off talking to Sara about her mindless and nasty behaviour. Good friends want their friends to get on; bad friends want to be the centre of their friends' lives and therefore don't want their friends to like each other.

Being piggy-in-the-middle can be just as bad as being the odd one out in a friendship. What do you do if your friends hate each other and you're being made to feel like you have to choose between them? Well, it's simple – don't choose. You're entitled to be friends with whoever you want. People who can't cope with this situation are being manipulative and destructive.

Sometimes it just happens that your friends don't get on. There may be a little possessiveness involved, maybe even a touch of jealousy. Best thing to do is to encourage your friends to at least tolerate each other. If you have no luck, then you'll just have to arrange to meet your friends at different times.

There is also a chance that the friction could be caused by you. You might have shown different aspects of your personality to each of your friends. Some might know you as an all-night party girl, while others know you as a quiet bookworm. In this situation, you have something in common with your friends, but your friends have nothing in common with each other. So before you start getting heavy with your friends, make sure that you are not the unwitting source of trouble.

Surviving a shared friendship

1 Don't play your friends off against each other.

2 Reassure jealous friends that you like them and that they are not to feel threatened by your other friends.

3 Every friendship is unique, and to each and every one of your friendships you bring something different.

4 If you are worried that a close friend has other friends, why not go out and get some more friends of your own. This is not some kind of tit-for-tat gesture but a really practical way to nip possessiveness in the bud.

FORMING A CLIQUE – Cliques are horrible things. Unlike big groups of friends who hang out together because they genuinely like each other, cliques are run along the lines of a very private 'members only' club. Yuk! They have strict rules about who is fit to join and they even have a kind of unofficial uniform. They may, for example, wear their hair in the same style, wear identical shoes and they usually wear the same sort of snarl.

If you're part of a clique you probably hate everything I've said so far, but it has to be accepted that a group of people who think that they are more sophisticated, cleverer or richer than everybody else has got to be bad news.

"Kate and I were best friends when we started secondary school but within a few weeks our relationship changed. Kate got in with the 'in' crowd because her dad works for a record company. She tried to get me in but they said I wasn't cool enough. They even had the nerve to say that they might let me in if I worked on my appearance. I was so mad that I told Kate that I didn't want to be friends with girls like that. I thought she'd stick by me, but she didn't – she chose them."
Marie, 15

Girls like the ones Marie described are not good-friend material. They ignore important qualities like loyalty, compassion, tolerance and character when choosing their friends, preferring instead to select their friends on the basis of who they are and what they look like.

If you're being excluded by such a group, be grateful that you do not have to keep their company. When I was at school there was one of these how-much-did-it-cost/who-do-you-go-out-with cliques, and me and my friends secretly wanted to be a part of it. We were, of course, excluded because we wore off-the-rack clobber and none of us had boyfriends!

While my friendships have survived through the years, the members of this clique have turned against each other. This proves that their idea of friendship was a total farce.

Real friends wouldn't contemplate laying down the law about who you can and can't be friends with. If your parents, for example, tried to tell you who you could and couldn't see, you'd be furious. So why should you tolerate it from the members of a clique?

"People think it's really good to be in with a crowd, but it's not. For instance, two of my friends don't like this boy in my class but I quite like him. They've told me that if I have anything to do with him they'll drop me. I tried to stick up for myself but I knew it was useless."

Sam, 15

<u>Good reasons for not being in a clique:</u>

1 You'll been seen as an individual rather than as part of a crowd.

2 You can do whatever you want and be friends with anyone you want.

3 People will like you for you and not for any other reason.

4 You don't have to be responsible for the actions of others.

GOSSIPING – Do you have friends who tell everyone your secrets? Do they spread malicious lies about you? Are you afraid to tell them anything in case it becomes fodder for the gossip mill? If any of these ring true, then you are at the mercy of scandalmongers.

People who do things like this are not good friends. You can't rely on them or trust them because you never know what they're going to say about you. In fact, because they like to gossip so much you can't even be sure that they're going to tell the truth about you.

"Louise is a brilliant friend but she just can't keep her mouth shut. This means that I can't tell her things. This upsets her because she says she tells me everything. I've told her why I don't trust her but she says she can't help it."
Elaine, 16

If you're a gossiping so-and-so who just can't keep your mouth shut, consider the following:

1 You're ruining your friendships and getting a bad reputation.

2 No one will trust you if you constantly spill the beans about others.

3 Your gossiping about others is a sign that you're not very happy with yourself and your life.

4 Imagine the tables were turned, and someone was spreading rumours about you. Can you imagine how hurt you would be?

*"I am a terrible gossip, but the worse thing I ever did
was tell some kids that my friend was moody because she
had skipped a period. The next thing I knew was that a story
about her being pregnant had done the rounds. My friend was so
upset and she kept asking who could have been so mean as
to start such a horrible story. I still live in fear that she
will find out it was me."*
Tammy, 15

If you've made a blunder like Tammy, don't make matters worse by feigning innocence – you've got to tell the truth. And don't try to wriggle out of it by saying "I didn't realise it was a secret" or "That's not what I said". The only thing you can say is "I'm sorry" and mean it. While it may make you feel popular to have people hanging on your every gossipy word, it won't get you any friends nor will it win you any respect.

USING PEOPLE – In a way we all use people. We use them to have fun with and to make us feel better. However, there is a different kind of using, and it is employed by only the most despicable examples of humankind. Users take what they want, give absolutely nothing in return, and then they leave you high and dry. Users have no morals. Read on to see what happened to Rachel.

*"Sarah and I were friends from the moment we met.
I thought she was really kind because she would invite me to
parties and to the cinema. The trouble was, the minute we got
anywhere she would desert me and go off with a boy or another
girl. It was weird because she'd beg me to come and then she'd
ignore me all night. Then she started ignoring me at school too,
but whenever she wanted to go somewhere she'd come on all
friendly. I felt too pathetic to complain so I let this go on for
months. Finally a girl in my class asked me why I let her
use me. She said Sarah hated going places on her own
and this is why she had attached herself to me."*
Rachel, 15

Rachel has described just one way a person can use and abuse a friendship, but there are other ways. They:

- ☛ borrow money with no intention of ever paying it back
- ☛ constantly borrow your clothes
- ☛ ask if they can copy your work
- ☛ lean on you but refuse to help you when you need it

If any of these sound familiar or you suspect your friends are using you, you need to deal with it by talking about it with your friends. Being used isn't good for your self-esteem. It leaves you feeling guilty and willing to accept the blame for what has happened. Often you will even punish yourself for letting it happen. What you've got to remember is that you don't have a problem, your friends do. If they are willing to change, terrific. If not, you're better off without them.

CHAPTER **four**

The best of friends

When I was eight years old I didn't have a best friend, I had lots of friends but there was no one with whom I shared 'that' special bond. I had a feeling that I should have a best friend; all the characters in the books I read had a special friend, kids in films were always having adventures with their best mate, most of the girls in my class seemed to have a best friend, and I even suspected that my mum and dad had special friends. So why didn't I? Instead of cruising the High Street in my laced-edged ankle socks and begging someone to be my best friend, I settled back and hoped that a best friend would knock on my door ending my friendless dilemma. Surprise, surprise – no one did.

Fast forward four years to when I was twelve. From having no best friend, I now had a new best friend every other month. I'd take a shine to someone, hang out with them, and tell everyone how we were going to be bosom-buddies for life. But within weeks I would go off them or they would go off me and that would be the end of that relationship. It wasn't a big deal – all us girls seemed to be doing it. Maybe these particular friendships weren't very deep or meaningful, or maybe we all mistakenly assumed that every friend should be a best friend.

When I reached my teens I thought I had the best friend racket sussed, but I was wrong. A few of my supposed best friends let me down and went off with other people or ditched me for a hunky (or sometimes not-so-hunky) boyfriend. Sometimes I was the guilty party. I'd make new friends and dump the old ones, or I would let my friends' annoying habits eat away at me until I couldn't hold back my temper. A rip-roaring argument would ensue and I would storm off in a huff. Broken friendships were the name of the game back then and I began to think that having best friends wasn't everything that it was cracked up to be.

After many false starts I have finally worked it out. I have four girl friends whom I consider to be my best friends. Our relationships developed slowly over a long period of time, and trust and loyalty abound. This means that none of my mates gets the hump if a) I don't see them for a while; b) I don't invite them to every event; c) I get cranky with them; or d) I don't return their calls pronto. We all understand that time and distance will not damage the special bonds that tie us together. But when we do get together it is terrific. Sometimes we talk about really serious matters of the heart ("Oh, why doesn't he love me?") and the State, at other times the conversation is so banal as to be frightening ("Would Superman be a good date?").

And what makes these four girls my best friends? They bring out the best in me. There is no role-playing, no deception and no competition for favours.

"My best friend is like a sister to me, but closer. I tell her everything that comes into my head, even the stupid things."
Carla, 15

"My best friend is the only person who really understands me."
Jo, 15

"My best friend is the first person I turn to when something terrible or wonderful happens."
Tina, 15

"Once when my boyfriend was treating me really badly, my best friend went up to him and told him to shape up or get out!"
Kelly, 14

THE BEST FRIENDS CHECKLIST

- ☛ they are your number one fan
- ☛ they bring out the best in you
- ☛ they aren't afraid to tell you off
- ☛ they stick around to pick up the pieces of a broken heart/lousy hair day/mega argument with the folks
- ☛ they want to do nice things for you
- ☛ they will do anything they can to help you out of a jam
- ☛ they can make fun of you and you won't be offended
- ☛ they stick up for you (even when they know you're wrong)
- ☛ they'll watch you try on fifty pairs of jeans until you find one pair that makes you happy
- ☛ they help you to see why you're so brilliant

Do you have to have best friends?

Having just sung the praises of having best friends, the next question has to be: Are best friends essential? The answer is: It depends on you. Some girls don't need or want to have just one best friend or even two or three best friends. They are happy hanging out with a whole crowd of people without declaring some of them to be 'special' friends.

"I don't have a best friend because I don't want one. I want to hang out with lots of people. I see my sister with her best friend and they're so annoying. They have all these in-jokes and secrets. It's no wonder that no one wants to hang out with them."

Lou, 15

"I used to have a best friend. But when she moved to another town I was left all alone. I'd spent so long just being friends with her that I didn't know anyone else. It took me ages to persuade people that I was worth getting to know. Now I have a group of friends not just one special friend."
Tina, 15

"Best friends are trouble. They make you look cliquey and stop other people from getting to know you. I don't understand girls who just stick to one or two really close friends. Don't they need the company of other people? What would they do if they fell out with their best friends? People are better off being friends with lots of people."
Dawn, 14

There's a lot of sense in what these girls are saying. Having one or two best friends can be asking for trouble. As Dawn points out, what happens if you fall out or your friends move? This is why it's best to have a number of best friends who you like and care about. There is nothing wrong with not having a special friend.

For some, the most natural best friends in the world are members of their own family.

"I have never felt the desire to have a best friend. I think that's because my sister is my closest friend. We have the kind of relationship that I know I won't find anywhere else."
Sharon, 17

The best friend syndrome

When you decide to choose just one person from among a crowd of friends to be your best friend, this can affect your relationships with other people. To declare that you've got a best friend is admitting that you prefer them to everyone else. Though you may not see it like this, your other friends will. Their feelings will be hurt and they may even start to compete for your attention.

"I know I'm not Lara's best friend and that hurts because I really like her. I'm always trying to prove that I'm as good as her best friend Rosie, but I know that whatever I do it won't change the connection they have. I don't think I'll ever have a best friend with whom I can share that special bond."

Sophie, 16

Best friends can cause trouble for other friends. Because of Sophie's problem with Lara, Sophie feels bad about herself. The only way to go if you want or already have one to two really special friends is to keep it quiet. There's no need to shout about it from the roof tops. You and your best friends know that your relationships are special, so who else really needs to know? In this way you can maintain other valuable friendships without hurting or offending anyone.

Some of you may think this sounds sort of sneaky, as if you're trying to have the best of both worlds — best friends and 'other' friends. Let me assure you, this is no underhand trick. Good friends don't have to brag about their friendship, because it's something that's inside them.

How to keep friends and best friends happy

1 Make sure your other friends don't feel left out.

2 Whether you choose to have best friends or not, there should always be enough space in your life to have lots of friends.

3 Don't do everything with your best friends. Get out and mingle with the rest of the world.

4 See people on your own. There's nothing more annoying than seeing girls who are seemingly joined at the hip.

5 Have your own views.

6 Don't quote your best friends all the time.

7 Don't always put your best friends first. If they are best friends, they will understand that you sometimes need to put others first.

How do people become best friends?

You can forget about magic potions and bribery – they won't help you to turn friends into best friends. Best friend relationships can't be rushed, nor taken lightly. They take time and everyone has to put in some effort.

I'm not sure how my relationships with my four best friends came about, they just sort of evolved naturally. One started as a letter-writing friendship when one friend moved to another country. We kept in contact via mail for two years, and when she came back to the UK it was as though she had never been away. In fact, the friendship had become even stronger.

Another of my best friends was originally someone I disliked with a passion. We either ignored or griped at each other until one day we both laughed ourselves hoarse all the way through a film. When we left the cinema, we left as friends. In time we became best friends.

I realised that another of my friends was really a best friend when she spent an entire day passing me tissues. I had just broken up with a boyfriend and could do nothing else but sob and snuffle. But did my friend leave me to be miserable alone? No, she stuck by me.

What I'm trying to say is that best friend relationships don't materialise overnight; they are ordinary friendships that grow into something very special. Sometimes they result from seemingly trivial happenings; sometimes it is a life-changing event that turns a casual friendship into a serious one.

"I knew we were all going to be best friends on the day we bought each other identical presents wrapped in the same paper."
Lisa,15

"I realised she was my best friend on the day my mum died because she came round and sat with me all day."
Kelly, 15

"Why are we best friends? I have no idea – she just makes me laugh."
Liz, 15

Have you got what it takes to be a best friend?

We've spent a lot of time looking at what best friend relationships can do for you, now it's time to see what sort of a best friend you will make. Do this easy-as-pie quiz to find out.

1 You're out shopping with a friend. She tries on a dress that makes her look gorgeous and asks your opinion. What do you say?

a You look like a supermodel. Buy it!

b Er ... do you like it?

c It's not really you.

2 Your friend and you both fancy the same guy. He approaches you and asks for her number. What do you do?

a Pretend you don't have it. After all, all's fair in love and war.

b Give him the number and leave it at that.

c Give him the number and drop a big hint that your friend really likes him.

3 Your friend complains that she hates Valentine's Day because she never gets any cards. What do you do?

a Suggest that you both have an anti-Valentine's Day.

b Try and make her feel better by showing her all your cards.

c Send her an anonymous card and never tell her it was from you.

4 Your friend calls you to ask you round because she's feeling lonely and miserable, but you and your boyfriend have a date. What do you do?

a Go on the date and see her tomorrow.

b Suggest she comes with you and your boyfriend.

c Postpone your date and see your friend.

5 Your friend tells you she has an eating disorder. What do you do?

a Say nothing because you don't want to get involved.

b Talk to her about it but agree to keep her secret.

c Talk to her mum.

Scores

1 a 10	b 5	c 0
2 a 0	b 5	c 10
3 a 10	b 0	c 5
4 a 0	b 5	c 10
5 a 0	b 5	c 10

Results

0 –15

You are going to have to learn to think about putting the needs of someone else first. Being a best friend means being there for your friends and wanting the best for them – it's not about competing against them.

And by the way, being a best friend is not something you do to fill in the time before you get a boyfriend.

20 – 40
Well, you're halfway to being best friend material. The only problem is that you have to be yourself a bit more. When you are with your best friends you shouldn't be afraid to express your opinions, or to admit that you don't like what's going down. Best friend relationships survive because of honesty.

45 – 50
Well, you're A-grade, super best friend material! You've probably got hundreds of friends already lined up! Honesty, respect and generosity – you've got the lot in abundance.

"My best friends have left me!"

Sometimes friendships – even good ones – end. If you're lucky they'll just peter out slowly and no one will be hurt. But if the friendship comes to a nasty, sticky end, the chances are that everyone involved will be feeling pretty awful.

What you've all got to remember is this: just because the relationship failed, it doesn't mean that you and your ex-friends are failures.

Most broken friendships are caused when friends simply grow away from each other, and not because someone did the dirty on someone else. So, okay this doesn't make you feel any better but it does mean that you can stop blaming yourselves and each other.

Coping with friendship downers

1 Learn to let go. If your friends think it is time to part, then accept their decision. If you try to force them back into the relationship, it will come to no good.

2 Don't live in the past and think about how it used to be. This will only make you miss the relationship and your friends even more. It will also stop you from moving on to find other friends and interests.

THE BEST OF FRIENDS

3 Don't start bitching or gossiping about your old friends. You will become bitter and twisted and then no one will want to know you.

4 Grieve for the lost friendship. This means talking about it, being angry, crying and then getting over it.

> *"Tina and I had been best friends for years, and then one day I came into school and she was with this other girl. She started sitting next to her and having lunch with her. I kept asking what I'd done but she'd just shrug her shoulders and walk off. It was awful – I felt so rejected."*
> Wendy, 16

> *"Kate and I have been going our separate ways for quite a while, but Kate won't let go. She doesn't want to do the same things as me but she always comes along because she thinks she should. This usually ruins things for me because I feel responsible for her."*
> Fran, 16

If you want to end a friendship and do it in the kindest and least hurtful way possible, follow this four point plan.

1 Make a clean break. Don't let feelings of remorse make you restart the friendship only to end it again.

2 Don't just abandon your friend or friends, they deserve to be told the truth.

3 Don't let guilty feelings make you stay in a friendship that is going sour. There is nothing to say that best friend relationships have to last for ever.

4 Keep some sort of friendship going with your old mates even if it's on a very casual level.

CHAPTER **five**

Friends who are bullies

Surely it's not possible, you think, for a friend to be a bully – but it is. And what's even sadder is that it is surprisingly common. Lots of people have friends who bully them and make their lives a total misery, but because they think their horrible situation is unique they hide it from others.

"I really didn't think anyone else had a friend like Pam. She was so mean and nasty. She'd pick on me, make me give her things and generally make my life hell. It was awful because my parents thought she was my best friend so they'd invite her everywhere. I lost count of the number of times I cried because I was frightened of her. Even though I haven't seen Pam for years the thought of her makes me want to be sick."
Caroline, 18

Anyone who has ever seen someone being bullied, or has been bullied themselves will know how terrifying and awful it is. Many, like Caroline, can remember years later about how humiliating and distressing it was. In fact, many bullied people find themselves suffering from lack of confidence well into their adult years. This occurs because a natural response to bullying is to blame yourself for letting it happen.

"Alison was very good at making me think it was all my fault. She'd bully me into something and then when I got upset she'd say it was all my idea. She got me so confused that I thought I must be imagining what was happening."
Claire, 15

If you're being bullied you are innocent and blameless. No one 'asks' or deserves to be bullied, no matter what the bully says. If you have a deep suspicion, hard evidence or even just a niggling feeling that you are being bullied, then you've got to keep your distance from the bully. No matter what tricks the bully plays to keep you within their power, you mustn't be tempted to hang in there – it's not worth the risk. There is no use keeping your fingers crossed and hoping that the bully will have a change of heart or that the tormenting will suddenly stop, because it's most unlikely.

Leaving a bully to get on with their reign of viciousness does not make you a bad friend. Reuniting with a friend who has really reformed would make you one mega-good friend. .

What bullies do

ERODE YOUR CONFIDENCE – When friends say mean things that dent your self-esteem and self-confidence it is hard not to be affected by what they say. After all, they are your friends and you trust and believe them.

"People ask why I listened to her for all that time. Well, I listened because she was my friend and I trusted her. I thought she had my best interests at heart and would never do anything to hurt me – but I was wrong. She persuaded me that I was rubbish at everything and that she was my only true friend. I've lost count of the number of dates I turned down on her advice. She'd say things like: you're not pretty enough for him or he's cleverer than you. It was only when I went away for the summer that I realised how happy and contented I was without her constant bullying."

Jenny, 15

Often a bully will use their hold over you to satisfy some selfish ulterior motive or to protect a secret. Allie's bully-friend worked her nastiness so that Allie would be without a boyfriend like herself.

"Every time I got a boyfriend Cassie was nasty. One time she told me that my boyfriend would have an affair because I was so dull. Another time she said that all my boyfriends flirted with her behind my back. I tried not to believe her but if someone says something often enough you start believing them. Eventually I realised that her tactics were more to do with the fact she had never had a boyfriend. I tried to talk to her about it but she accused me of being jealous. At that point I realised there was no point being friends with her any more."

Allie, 16

Meanness and self-interest are not a natural part of any friendship. If you recognise that one of your friends is a bully, you have every right to be

angry. The bully has deceived you – they have masqueraded as a friend. You can try talking about it with her, but if talking changes nothing then it's time to say 'Hasta la vista, baby' and quit the relationship. Friends who hurt you aren't friends.

TELL LIES – Bullies will tell lies about you in order to gain control, get you into deep trouble and to isolate you from your other friends.

"Annie is always telling lies about me. She tells people I am really into sex when she knows I am a virgin. While I'm getting into trouble because of her lies, she plays Miss Innocent. My other friends have said that I should either chill out or simply see less of her. But they don't realise that with me or without me, Annie will still tell lies. When I try to talk to her about it she says I'm imagining everything."

Helen, 16

The trouble with lies is that one lie always leads to another and another, and before you know it you're caught in a very sticky web. What may have seemed initially like harmless exaggerations snowball out of control with you caught helpless and hapless in the middle.

There is a way out and that's to tell the truth. Don't let a sense of misplaced loyalty stop you from spilling the beans about the bully and telling everyone the facts. After all, a lying bully isn't exactly a model of loyalty themselves. If people try to persuade you that you're over-reacting, ignore them.

After you have repaired your reputation by setting everyone straight, confront the liar. Tell them you're happy with the truth about your life and that it needs no embellishing. If they keep doing it, keep away from them.

TAKE YOUR THINGS – All friends borrow things from each other, but good friends do not take your stuff with the intention of never returning it. Only bullies do this.

"Louise used to borrow things from me all the time. At first I didn't mind because I thought she was a good friend and I was happy to share my stuff. But she never returned anything and when she started nicking money I knew that I had to put a stop to it. I was afraid to confront her so I tried to sort it out myself. It was then that I found out that she'd played the same con trick on three other girls."
Janey, 15

If you are in the same predicament as Janey you must stand up for yourself. Someone who takes things without permission is a thief. You may think that this is a harsh description but this is what she is – a common thief.

Think about it, you wouldn't walk into someone's house and just take their things would you? And if you wouldn't do that, why should you let a 'friend' get away with it?

If you can't confront your friend, talk to your parents. If they have taken something that you want back, ask your parents to step in and retrieve it for you. This will kill two birds with one stone. It will let your friend know that the game's up and you'll get all your stuff back. What happens to the friendship is up to you. You may think the friendship is worth saving or you may be happy to simply turn your back on it.

"My best friend bullies me"

This is one of the saddest situations of all. Imagine your best friend, someone you trust and care about, bullying you. It must be so frightening.

Victims of bullies rarely say anything because it is almost impossible to admit (even to themselves) that they are being abused by a so-called best friend. Often people in such a relationship feel trapped, scared and afraid to do anything. They most probably have to see their tormentor day in and day out, sit next to them in class, have lunch with them, and all the time they're having to put on a brave face. The victims of best-friend bullies can rarely see any escape from the horrible trap.

"Angie was my best friend and also my worst enemy. Every day for five years she made me miserable. She'd walk me to school, and then stick by my side all day. This meant I could never get away from her and her demands. I was so afraid of her that I did everything she said. The other girls used to make fun of me because they said I was her slave – they couldn't have been more right. As a result I became very shy and withdrawn. My parents kept asking me what was wrong but I couldn't tell them what was going on. I lived in fear of them finding out that I was weak and unable to stand up for myself. I hated myself for letting Angie do this to me. She ruined my school years totally and it took me years to get over what she'd done."
Sophie, 23

How to spot a bully

1 Do you feel scared of your friend?

2 Are you afraid to express your opinions in her presence?

3 Does she force you into doing things that you don't want to do?

4 Do you wish she would move away?

5 Do you pretend to be sick so that you don't have to see her?

6 Do you lie to protect her?

7 Do you try to excuse her behaviour as harmless teasing?

8 Are you putting her demands before everything else because you're terrified not to?

9 Do you feel panicky when you're going to see her?

10 Do any of your classmates or other friends comment on your friend's behaviour?

Any of the above are a sign that you're being bullied. The only way to put an end to it is to speak out to a trusted adult.

Telling your story and convincing an adult that you are telling the honest truth can be hard. Very often there is no evidence or any witnesses. But you must keep telling your story until someone acts on it. In the meantime, you will have to make a big effort to stay well away from the bully and in the company of other people. Tell your parents because they can make sure the bully leaves you alone at home.

Despite all the publicity about bullying, some schools are still unable to put a stop to it. If your friend is bullying you at school and the teachers are not doing anything to help, your parents can write to the school governors and to the Local Education Authority. If the situation threatens to result in physical harm, your parents can contact the police.

> For help and advice contact:
> **ABC (Anti Bullying Campaign)**
> 10 Borough Street, London SE1.
> Tel: 0171 378 1446
>
> **Childwatch**
> 206 Hessle Road, Hull,
> North Humberside HU3 3BE.
> Tel: 0482 25552
>
> **Kidscape**
> 152 Buckingham Palace Road, London SW1W 9TR
> Tel: 0171 730 3300
>
> **Childline**
> Freephone: 0800 1111

Why does someone become a bully ?

Though it is very hard to have any sympathy for a bully, there are things that can drive someone to adopting bullying behaviours. For these people, bullying is their way of overcoming or concealing other personal problems like shyness, compulsive lying and low self-esteem.

FRIENDS WHO ARE BULLIES

"I can't help lying"

For some bullies, lying is an automatic reaction. They find it impossible to give a straight, honest answer to a straight question. Bullies will also put themselves into situations where they have to tell lies. The only way they can put a stop to this sort of behaviour is if they think before they open their mouths. They will have to learn to ask themselves these sorts of questions: Do I really need to lie about this? What's to be gained? Who will it hurt? What sort of trouble will this cause? When they look at the situation like this, there's no way that they could tell a lie.

> *"I'm always showing off to my friends and telling
> lies. I just can't help it. I'm not even sure why I do it.
> All I know is one friend will tell me something and I'll have
> to go one better. I feel really bad about lying because I know
> I shouldn't be so competitive with my friends. The biggest lie I
> told got my best friend into trouble. She got higher marks than me
> in an exam and I told everyone she'd cheated. Our teacher
> found out and she had to do the test again. It was a lie
> but I couldn't bring myself to admit it."*
> Sara, 16

If a bully has used lying as a way of keeping their friends under their control, then their friends are going to have to let it be known that until the fruitless and nasty lying stops, the friendships must end. The bully will soon get the message: if they want to have any friends, they will have to stick to the truth.

"I'm shy"

Believe it or not shyness can make someone a bully. This is how it happens: to express her frustration at being shy and lacking in confidence, the bully is mean and rotten to her friends. The oh-so-tough behaviour totally masks her insecurities, and puts everyone off wanting to know her better. She fears that if people got to know her, then she would have to open up to them and reveal her lack of self-esteem. For some reason bullies think it is easier to be nasty than nice.

"Inside I'm really scared about everything, but I'm even more frightened of letting people see the real me. So what I do is act tough and assertive. Unfortunately, I go over the top. I've reduced my best friends to tears and have been told that I am a bully. I hate it that I have given people the wrong impression. I'm not really a bully, just terribly scared."
Jackie, 16

If the bully wants to break the nasty cycle of fear-driven bullying – she will have to reveal her true self. It will take guts because those who have suffered under her reign of bullying may take advantage of the situation for some not-so-sweet revenge. But if she is committed to making the change, she will endure the scorn and derision that may come her way. What she has to understand is that good, close friendships are based on honesty and trust, not on terror tactics. Once she reveals her true personality and makes amends for being such a heel, true friendships will be just around the corner. And when they do come, she'll wonder why she ever resorted to bullying!

"No one likes me"

When people believe that no one likes them, it's easy to lash out and hate everyone in return.

"No one ever gives me a chance to be a friend so why should I be nice to them. People think I'm trouble, so I don't disappoint them. Sometimes I wish they'd see me for who I really am, but I don't think anyone's ever going to give me a chance."
Suzanne, 16

If someone thinks that they are the odd one out or assumes that everyone hates them, then becoming the outsider or being disliked soon becomes a self-fulfilling prophecy. They bully people, and in return they are ostracised and hated, and so the spiral continues.

But it is possible for the bully to put their reputation behind them and to start again. It won't be easy but it will be worth it. The bully will have to work at not being mean, and will have to go overboard on being friendly. In time people will see that a bully can change its spots!

CHAPTER **six**

Boys as friends and boyfriends

How do you feel about having a boy as a friend? Does it make you want to stick two fingers down your throat, or does the idea of a purely platonic relationship with a male of the species hold some appeal? Some of you may be wondering what on earth you'd talk about with a boy; others may be more concerned about what everyone else will be talking about behind your back!

> *"Jim is my best friend, though many people find that hard to believe. There is always someone trying to spread a rumour that Jim is gay, that I'm a tree-climbing tomboy, or that Jim and I are having an affair. I just can't believe that people are so narrow-minded. Why can't they accept that Jim is my best friend. Surely it doesn't matter where you find friendship?"*
> Lisa, 15

One of the many good things about having a boy as a friend is that you get a chance to understand the male perspective. You can learn what makes them tick, how they see things and what really annoys them. Susan and Paul have been friends since they were ten years old.

*"Paul's great because he helps me when I'm
confused about boys. For instance, there was this
boy who I knew really liked me, but he wouldn't ask me out.
I didn't know what to do until Paul showed me how unfair it was
that girls always waited for guys to ask them out. I thought
about it and decided Paul was right. I asked this guy out
and we're still dating. Thanks, Paul."*
Susan, 16

A boy-girl friendship can be just as rewarding for the boy. He can get all
the inside info on the female psyche.

*"Being friends with Susan has helped me to understand
girls and why they do the things they do. I know my male friends
think our friendship is really weird. They think it's impossible to be
friends with a girl without fancying her. It doesn't bother me that
they think like this; it's their loss not mine."*
Paul, 16

The perils of having a male friend

The down-side to having a boy as a friend is that a very genuine
friendship can be put under a lot of stress by thoughtless comments,
misconceptions and the presence of the green-eyed monster.

NASTY GOSSIP – Having a male friend gets tongues wagging like
nothing else and in the end can cause the friendship to collapse.

When I was at school I had a good friend who was a boy. We hung
out together, did our homework together, and shared all those things that
good mates share. There was nothing else to our relationship – no secret
snogging and absolutely no intention of ever snogging. But our friends
were always on to us: Are you really dating? Do you hold hands? When
we said no to all their prying questions, they looked at us as if we were
decidedly odd. What we couldn't explain was that our feelings for each
other were totally different to the sort of feelings we would have for
people we wanted to date.

Fifteen years later and I still find it difficult to clearly explain the subtle difference between having a boyfriend and having a boy as a friend.

Eventually the strain of coping with all this thoughtless interference got too much. We started feeling awkward in each other's company – each one secretly thinking that the other wanted to make more of this friendship than they were saying. Sadly, we were too scared to talk about our feelings and we drifted apart. A good friendship was lost for ever.

What we should have done was talked about the niggling problem and cleared the air. Then we could have done something to nip the gossip in the bud. As it was, the rumours grew and grew until the most amazing stories were flying around. Even my normally tolerant mum and dad were getting a bit worried about the situation!

If a similar set of circumstances is threatening to spoil one of your friendships then you both have to stand up and defend your relationship. If people ask if you and your male friend are really dating, turn the question back on them. Ask them why they aren't mature enough to handle the fact that people of the opposite sex can have a caring and trusting relationship without love, lust or sex being involved. Money on, your interrogator will be flummoxed – they won't know what to say.

JEALOUSY – The green-eyed monster makes an appearance in most friendships sooner or later, but a girl-boy friendship is susceptible on two fronts. Firstly, one of you may become jealous when the other starts to date. Secondly, the new-on-the-scene girl- or boyfriend may be just a tad jealous of your unusual relationship.

"When Steve got a girlfriend I was really happy for him and I couldn't wait to meet her. But, boy did I regret it! Gia spent the whole night holding on to Steve's arm and kissing him. She kept saying how weird it was that I hung around Steve all the time. She made me feel like I was some sort of pathetic charity case. If Steve hadn't come round to apologise the next day, I don't think I would have spoken to him again."
Tara, 16

If your boyfriend is behaving in a similar way to Steve's girlfriend, then it's your responsibility to fix the situation. You owe it to your friendship to put an end to such unnecessary nastiness.

There are a number of ways to deal with a jealous and thoughtless girlfriend or boyfriend. The first step is for you to realise that they are acting this way because they feel threatened. They know that you two most probably go back a long time, have shared many things and have already established a trusting relationship. The girlfriend or boyfriend is threatened by this cosy and secure relationship. What they then do is try to compete by emphasising the physical aspect of their relationship. That's why Gia kept pawing Steve – she was showing Tara that Steve was her property and that Tara had better back off. Read Gia's letter to see her side of the story.

"I knew Steve had this female friend who he really liked and it really upset me. I sort of got the feeling that I was second-best. So when I met Tara I behaved appallingly. I wanted her to know that it was time she left Steve alone."
Gia, 16

So, the second step for you to take is to reassure the girlfriend that she has nothing to fear. Explain that as a friend you can think of nothing nicer than for your friend to be dating. This will make it patently clear that the relationship you have is purely platonic.

When friendship turns to love

Strange things often happen in friendships and someone who you once viewed as 'just a friend' suddenly becomes that 'someone special'.

"Tim and I had been best mates for years. Then I realised that I really fancied him in a boyfriend-type of way. I didn't tell him for ages because I thought he'd freak out. I finally bought it up and he said, 'Thank godness, I've fancied you for ages!'"
Mel, 17

If both of you are into having a relationship that's great because it means that your relationship will be off to a good start. After all, you already know each other very well, and you both know how not to get on each other's nerves.

Problems only occur if the feeling is not mutual. If this happens, then don't pretend that these emotions don't exist. This will only lead to you feeling hurt, depressed and jealous when your friend starts to date someone else.

The best way to handle this situation is to be frank. Tell your friend how you feel. What happens to your friendship will depend on you both: you accepting that anything more than friendship is impossible, and him being able to realise that nothing has really changed. You are, after all, the same person that has been his friend for many years. Falling in love is something that just happens – you've done nothing wrong.

Getting over unrequited love is hard but you can make it easier on yourself by not seeing your friend so often (there is no need to break the friendship completely) and turning to other friends for comfort and advice.

How to reject a male friend's advances:

1 Be honest and up front, but nice. Don't forget he's still a friend and it's always worth trying to save a friendship.

2 Don't lock yourself in your bedroom and refuse to see him. This is hurtful and solves nothing.

3 Don't give him any false hopes. Explain why you can't see him as anything more than a good friend.

4 Don't feel bad about it.

5 If he suggests that you give the new relationship a go, be firm and say no. There's nothing worse than becoming involved in a relationship out of a sense of obligation and guilt.

6 Don't feel that he's let you down. He can't help being in love with you.

7 If he doesn't want to see you for a while, don't push it. He needs time to get over you, and this means time away from you.

Friends and boyfriends!

Well, this is when the boys, friends and love situation becomes very tricky. There's so much to consider when you first fall in love – your boyfriend's personality, your personality; his interests, your interests; and his friends, your friends. It's not easy to get the balance right between maintaining old friendships and starting a new one, especially one as exciting as a love relationship. It's like trying to juggle six balls without ever being taught how to do it. You know that if you drop one of those balls it may jeopardise your friendships and your relationship with your boyfriend. Like I said before, it's very tricky!

"I still wonder if Liz realises how badly she treated me. She never apologised for letting me down and as for my birthday, well, I can't forgive her for that. She promised that she would come out to celebrate with me and my family, and then she didn't bother to show up. I was so embarrassed and humiliated. She was supposed to be my best friend."
Sharon, 16

"I treated Sharon so badly when I started seeing Robert. I even missed her birthday because Robert came round unexpectedly. I guess I expected her to always be there."
Liz, 15

Taking a friend or a group of friends for granted like this is a recipe for disaster. Even the most loyal (and patient) friends in the world aren't going to play second fiddle to a boyfriend. It isn't nice for friends to suspect that they have just been filling-in while you waited for Mr Right to come skating along. It's also very hurtful for your friends to know that they're not considered as important as the boyfriend. It's perfectly easy to keep your friends and a boyfriend happy. All it takes is a bit of thought and planning.

Are you guilty of neglecting your friends?

Here are the danger signs to watch out for:
1 Are your friends dropping not-so-subtle hints that you're letting them down and being a bad friend?

2 Are major things happening in the lives of your friends that you know nothing about?

3 Have you forgotten important dates or failed to show up when you promised?

4 When you talk to your friends, what do you talk about?

5 When was the last time you had a girls-only outing?

Friends and boyfriends who don't get on

If it all goes horribly wrong between your boyfriend and your friends, try to be understanding. Your friends are anxious that they might lose you, and your boyfriend is fearful that the friends will try to break up the relationship. Your friends don't want to make your life difficult, they just need reassuring.

The following letters from Sally, Deb and Gary are about a nasty friendship triangle.

"I can't stand Deb's boyfriend, Gary. He's rude, he's opinionated and he thinks he's gorgeous. He's always trying to flirt with me and I hate it. I know Deb doesn't mind but I do!"
Sally, 15

"Sally is a complete cow and I think she's trying to split Deb and me up. I've really tried to be nice to her but when I do she acts as if I'm coming on to her. Now I just say what I want and I don't care if she likes me or not."
Gary, 16

"It's a complete nightmare when I'm out with Sally and Gary. Sally complains that he's rude, and Gary just laughs at her. Then they both get stroppy when I refuse to take sides. I like them both and I want them to be friends, but I don't know what to do."
Deb, 15

Deb has noticed all the danger signs of warring friends: they constantly bicker, they try to get you to take sides, they complain about each other, and they make no effort to get to know each other or to get along.

What to do

1 You have to accept that there is no law that says friends and boyfriends have to get along.

2 Don't force them to be in each other's company. See your friends and your boyfriend at different times.

3 Call a truce. Tell them that you understand how they all feel, and that you accept (unhappily, of course) the situation as it stands.

4 Tell them they don't have to like each other but they do have to be polite when you're around.

5 Refuse to discuss your friends with your boyfriend, and likewise don't talk about your boyfriend with your friends.

6 Don't take sides.

When friends are jealous of your new relationship

Personality clashes aside, there is a chance that your friends are a tad jealous of your new and intense relationship with a boy. This is made worse when your friendship with them has, until now, been one of 'all us girls together'. Many friendship groups have been formed because none of the friends had boyfriends. For ages you've all hung around together, had a great time and shared lots of giggles. Then suddenly, you get a boyfriend. The whole friendship group changes. It is no longer all of you against the world, but all of them against you.

Don't worry, things will get back to normal if you do the right thing. If you treasured the friendships then you'll do your utmost to keep them going. Once again, you just have to reassure your friends that your boyfriend makes no difference to your relationship with them.

What to do when the boyfriend is jealous

There are some people who would tell you thank your lucky stars for having a boyfriend who is so smitten. But I can tell you that a jealous and possibly possessive boyfriend is no different to a jealous friend (see page 41). Both will make your life a misery!

Even if you are head over heels in love with the boy, did you really expect to have to spend every minute of your day with him? Did you plan to ditch all your others friends so as to keep him happy? Not likely. The suffocating relationship that results from having a jealous boyfriend is not a good relationship.

To get your boyfriend to release his stranglehold on your social life, you have to do the following:

1 Talk to him about the problem. Make it clear to him (and I'm sure you will) that as a boyfriend he's wonderful, but as a friend he's the pits. Tell him that a good friend would never think of controlling a friend's life.

2 Reassure him that he is just as important as your friends. If you say that he's more important, you are playing right into his possessive hands.

3 Don't encourage any sort of jealous behaviour by playing your boyfriend off against your friends. The poor guy is obviously insecure and it wouldn't take much to really freak him out.

4 Let him know that what happens in your relationship is simply between you and him. If he suspects that you are blabbing the details of every snog to your friends, then is it any wonder that he's trying to keep you away from them?

5 If all this tact and diplomacy doesn't change your boyfriend's jealous behaviour then the relationship is doomed.

CHAPTER **seven**

Troublemakers

When I was fifteen I had a friend who was labelled trouble with a capital 'T'. In my eyes she was cool, but in the eyes of anyone older than seventeen she was bad news. She wore short, short skirts to school, smoked in the playground and went out with the toughest boy in the neighbourhood.

I don't know how we became friends, but I do know that I admired her courage to stand up for herself and desperately wanted to be like her. (Sort of an impossible aspiration as I didn't even have the guts to talk in assembly, let alone smoke in the playground.) Time and again I was warned to keep away from her.

Teachers told me that she would "bring me down to her level", and friends said that her bad reputation would rub off on me. But the crucial thing was, she wasn't anything like her reputation.

In fact, out of all my friends she was the one who kept me away from trouble. She didn't try to coax me into smoking or drinking, and it wasn't her who said that having sex was cool. She was the one who warned me about boys with wandering hands and taught me how to say no. She was my first lesson in not judging a book by it's cover.

That's the trouble with rumoured reputations – they're not reliable! More often than not they're a mixture of half-truths, exaggeration and gossip. I admit that my friend had a colourful past and had made some mistakes, but surely she didn't have to pay for them for the rest of her life? If only people had bothered to get beyond the stories and made the effort to get to know her.

When a reputation is deserved

Troublemakers don't always wear short skirts, have bad attitudes and have 'I am trouble' emblazoned on their T-shirts. Some bods hide their devious naughtiness under a cloak of pure angelic behaviour, and the only way to tell the good guys from bad guys is by how they behave towards you.

> *"My parents loved Elizabeth because she spoke nicely, came from a good home and always did the right thing in front of them. Pity it was all just an act. In reality and out of the sight of parents and teachers she was a right troublemaker. She took drugs, drank and slept around. And what's more, she wanted me to do the same things as her. When I refused she threatened to tell everybody that I was doing these things anyway. She was a nightmare and nobody knew it."*
> Stephanie, 16

If a friend lives up to her reputation, or secretly has one that's getting her and you into trouble there are a number of things you should do.

1 Protect yourself. Don't let a friend's behaviour put you in danger.

2 Protect her. If a friend gets into something that is dangerous and won't seek help, then seek help on her behalf.

3 If a friend chooses to cause trouble for herself, then you have a choice: help her, advise her or if all else fails walk away from her.

4 Don't lie for her.

5 Don't give her your approval.

6 If a so-called friend tries to tempt you into serious trouble or make trouble for you, then there's only one thing you can do – pack in the friendship before it's too late.

Peer pressure

What exactly is peer pressure? Well, it's when your friends try to encourage you to do something because they're doing it. Quite often it is something that is illegal or at the least bound to cause strife. It's important to understand why your friends are so eager for you to join them; it's not because they want you to be the same, but because they don't want you to be different.

These are the areas in which peer pressure is exerted: having sexual relationships, drinking alcohol, smoking, drug-taking, shoplifting, skiving off school, lying, and driving without a license.

Your friends might try to tempt you into these things by saying that you're a wuss or chicken if you don't. They may also give you the cold-shoulder and threaten to spread nasty gossip unless you do what they want you to do. These guys will sink really low to make sure that you are in a position where you can't say no.

If you have a friend or a group of friends who are trying to force you to break the law, take drugs or do anything else that you don't really want to do, you need to ask yourself this: Are these people really my friends? The only honest answer is 'no'.

Friends accept a person as they are, even if that person isn't like them in lots of ways. Friends don't want to lead you astray. Promise.

Pressured into having sexual relationships

Have any of your friends ever said any of the following to you?

"Everyone's doing it."
"It's unhealthy to be a virgin."
"You can't get pregnant the first time you have sex."
"He'll leave you if you don't."
"You must be frigid."
"You'll love it."

If they have, then you're not the first. These are classic peer pressure lines that were doing the rounds even when I was at school. Thing is, they're all giant porkies; there's not a grain of truth in any of them. The decision to have or to not have sex is a personal one. It's not something that is open to group discussion, nor is it an issue that should be decided by the mob. If you're being bullied by your friends into having sex with your boyfriend, remember these points:

1 Having sex is easy, it's living with the possible aftermath that is hard.

2 Get your information about sex from books, parents, trusted teachers and older siblings.

3 Sex can be great, exciting and fun at the right time with the right person, but it's also life threatening if you don't take precautions.

4 The age of consent is sixteen years old (seventeen years old in Northern Ireland). This means that it is against the law for any male to have sex with any girl who is under sixteen. This does not mean that when you are sixteen you must race out and have sex or can be forced into having sex. You have a right to say no, whatever your age.

Having sex because you want to be like your friends is bad news. The only reason you should ever have sex is if you're with someone you trust and care about, and you're a hundred per cent sure that you're doing it because you want to do it.

Pressured into drinking alcohol

Many people drink because they want to feel better about themselves and hope that an artificially-induced alcohol 'high' will do it for them. However, what most people don't realise is that alcohol is a depressant. The high is only temporary and once you come down you'll feel worse than you did before you drank. Then, of course, there's the mental and physical effects of drinking alcohol:

1 When you drink alcohol, the alcohol enters the bloodstream and reaches the brain within five minutes of being swallowed. In other words, the brain stops functioning normally and your judgement is impaired even before you've finished the first glass.

2 When you drink heavily you risk serious health problems: weight gain, dehydration, vomiting and last but not least you get a hangover. A hangover is another word for alcohol poisoning.

3 You can hurt yourself if you fall.

4 Twenty-five per cent of 13-17 year-olds get into fights after drinking.

5 One thousand children under the age of 15 are admitted to hospital each year with acute alcohol poisoning.

6 Twenty-five thousand people die a year as a result of alcohol abuse.

Remember these sobering facts when your friends try to force you to get drunk. It wouldn't hurt to remind them of the damage they are doing to themselves. To avoid this sort of peer pressure don't hang around with your friends when they are going on a binge and don't even hang around while they are planning a drinking session. If you are out with friends, always buy your own drinks. In that way you can buy soft drinks without anyone knowing and there is no chance of someone slipping you a spiked drink.

Pressured into smoking or taking other drugs

There are many ways friends might try to persuade you to smoke or take other drugs. They might tell you that they've tried it and it was 'great', 'safe' and 'made them look cool'. Your friends might be experimenting for the first time and they may suggest that it's time you experimented as well. Sometimes they want you to join in just so that you can help pay for the cigarettes and other drugs. Whatever their reasons, there's no getting away from the fact that smoking and other drugs are TROUBLE!

If you know what makes smoking and other drugs dangerous, it is much easier for you to resist peer pressure. Let's face it, who would willingly do something that they know might just as likely kill them on the spot or in a few years time.

Following is a guide to a few of the drugs you may be offered and why you should turn them down.

Speed

Also known as amphetamines, whizz, sulphate, A, uppers, pep pills, diet pills, jelly beans, ice, or crystal.

Dangers: Even at low doses, speed can cause dramatic mood swings, temper tantrums, irritability and restlessness. Taken regularly, speed can produce mental confusion, panic and paranoia. Users also end up becoming physically run down because of lack of sleep and an inadequate diet. These can cause everything from bad skin to anxiety attacks. The effects of speed can lead to a psychological dependence. This means that a person comes to rely on the drug to get them through many everyday situations. The prospect of being without that substance makes a person extremely anxious and depressed. High dose and long term use can lead to delusions, hallucinations and hostility, plus damaged blood vessels or heart failure.

Ecstasy

Also known as E, MDMA, XTC, Dennis the Menace, disco burgers, lovedoves, or M25s.

Dangers: Ecstasy is a rave drug that stimulates the nervous system and energises the muscles, which then allows a person to dance for hours and hours.

The most important danger to watch out for is dehydration or heat stroke. These occur because ecstasy causes the body's temperature to rise. This increase in body temperature along with increases in blood pressure are implicated in ecstasy deaths. E also causes exhaustion, teeth grinding, jaw clenching, anxiety attacks, depression and insomnia.

Ecstasy is rarely 'pure' these days and it is often mixed with speed, LSD, talcum powder and Ketamine. This means that you don't know what you're putting in your mouth, and what damage it will do to your body.

Cannabis

Also known as marijuana, hash, pot, grass, resin, dope, ganja, spliff, joint, wacky baccy, and blow.

Dangers: The biggest danger with cannabis is the state of intoxication that it induces. When stoned, regular users are more likely to be lethargic, unco-ordinated and unable to concentrate or perform everyday-type tasks to their best ability. This means that the likelihood of having an accident, especially when driving, crossing a road or using machinery, is increased.

Solvents

Also known as aerosols, glue, lighter fluid, S, and household cleaning products.

Dangers: While the effects of sniffing solvents is rather like getting drunk very quickly, the dangers are far greater. The high wears off faster, which means that within forty-five minutes of inhaling a user will be feeling pretty rough. The experience feels like a hangover and the user may well have a headache and feel tired. This mixed with constant headaches and nasty sores around the mouth and nose makes solvent abuse pretty unappealing. Likewise, the visual hallucinations that solvents can cause can be terrifying.

The most dangerous risks are sniffing until you pass out, or choking on your own vomit. These can occur even with first-time use. A person sniffing repeatedly will suffer from tiredness, forgetfulness and loss of concentration. There may also be weight loss, depression, and liver and kidney complaints. Deep inhalation causes drowsiness, numbness and unconsciousness. Massive misuse of aerosols and cleaning fluids also causes lasting kidney and liver damage.

For help and information call:
THE NATIONAL DRUGS HELPLINE
Freephone 0800 77 66 00

The phonelines are manned 24 hours a day.
The trained counsellors are friendly and sympathetic.
Everything is kept in the strictest confidence.

Pressured into shoplifting

Shoplifting is a nice way of saying stealing. If your friends are trying to con you into nicking stuff from a shop, consider the hard facts of being light-fingered.

1 Shop owners always prosecute and you could end up with a criminal record.

2 Your parents will definitely find out.

3 The price of goods rises directly as a result of shoplifting. To cover the money lost on stolen property, retailers make things more expensive.

4 You will be caught. Maybe not the first time or the second time, but eventually.

5 Even if you're not doing any actual shoplifting but your friends are, you will be dragged in with your friends when they get caught.

The simple way to avoid the whole issue is to simply refuse to go anywhere near the shops when you're with your friends. If they want to go 'shopping', you find something else to do.

Troublemakers and troubled parents

If your parents have a problem with one of your friends, you need to ask yourself whether they're right or not. Someone who is known for being in trouble with the police, or for drinking and taking drugs doesn't exactly inspire confidence in parents. However, if you think your friend has changed and deserves a second chance, then talk to your parents about it. Pretending to your parents that you're not seeing your friend will only prove to them that they were right – the friend is trouble.

"Kelly is my best friend and I love being with her. The problem is my parents hate her. They say she is leading me astray. They have forbidden me to see her, but I haven't told Kelly because I don't want to hurt her feelings. On the other hand, I don't want to lie to my parents by sneaking out to meet her. I don't know what to do."
Jane, 15

How to convince your parents that they've got it all wrong

1 Encourage them to let her come to your house so they can see that your friend has indeed changed and deserves a second chance.

2 Tell your parents the whole story of your friend's troubled past as you know it. It is quite likely that they may have heard only a very distorted version of the truth.

3 Abide by your parents' curfews and rules when you're with your friend.

If you can't get your parents to change their minds, then your only consolation is that they are trying to protect you. It's easy to understand how parents can over-react when the newspapers are full of stories about the perils of falling in with bad company.

Getting your parents to trust your friends

If you want your parents and your friends to get on, there are a number of things you can do to make life easier for yourself.
1 Give your parents lots of opportunities to meet your friends. One fleeting 'hello, nice to meet you, goodbye' is just not enough. If you hide your friends away it will make your parents very suspicious.

2 Write down your friends' telephone numbers and give the list to your parents. I know this idea stinks, but it will do wonders for your relationship with your parents. They will respect you for your maturity and they will trust you even more. Just knowing that they can find their daughter should an emergency arise does wonders for your parents' stress levels.

3 Let your parents know how sensible you are by talking to them about the things that they are worried about. For instance, tell them you're against drugs because you know the dangers, and that you can be trusted when there's alcohol around. Reassure them that you were listening when they gave you the lecture about the birds and the bees.

4 Don't always choose to do things away from home. Ask if you can have a party at your house or have friends to stay for a sleep-over. The more your parents get to know your friends the easier your life will be.

5 Don't be secretive. If you have whispered conversations on the telephone, arrange clandestine meetings with your friends in funny places, lock your room and refuse to look your parents in the eye, your parents will think you're up to no good. Can you blame them?.

6 Don't run your parents down when you're talking to your friends. For example, don't describe your parents as little better than modern-day Attila the Huns. Likewise don't tell your parents about how all your mates skived off from school and were nabbed by the truant police. Stuff like this won't endear your friends to your parents, or your parents to your friends.

eight

Friends in trouble

Traumas, trials and tribulations are always a major test of any friendship. I know plenty of self-professed good friends who have run a mile when things got too tough for their best mates. I also know plenty of good-time pals who disappear the second everything's not hunky-dory. While these types of friends have their place in the grand scheme of things, they aren't the kinds of friends that can be relied on. This is why it's always worth knowing who you can count on should anything hairy happen.

Hopefully nothing terrible will ever happen to you so you won't have to put your friendships to the big test, however, it's a good idea to know who your real mates are. So take a good hard look at them to see who would be at your side in a time of crisis. Which ones would drop everything if you were desperate? Which ones could keep their heads when everyone else is losing theirs? Which ones could maintain a positive attitude when everything seems negative? If you've got friends you can count on in any situation, then count yourself very, very fortunate.

The other side of the coin is this: How willing are you to be there for a friend with a major problem? Would you give a friend the right kind of help if they were in trouble? Do you know when to keep a secret? And more importantly, could you bring yourself to ask for help on their behalf and would you know who to approach?

It's good to listen

Being a good listener is very important. Good friends can listen without judging and without feeling that they have to take control. They know that there is a big difference between being supportive and taking matters into their own hands. Not all 'crises' require friends to don their Action Women outfits. Often all they have to do is sit still while they are being used as sounding-board.

If some action is required, then good friends will not just promise to do something, they will actually do it. They will even put their own necks on the chopping-block to help out. They may risk being grilled by their own parents or by the school counsellor when they seek help on their friend's behalf. But this is what good friends will do – they will go out of their way to see you right.

Good friends do not load themselves down with the problems of others. They don't go around feeling depressed as if they are carrying the problems of the world on their narrow shoulders. Instead they try to be upbeat and positive. Down-in-the-dumps friends aren't going to be of much help, are they?

If good friends (and I mean *good* friends) say that they are unable to help – maybe the problem is too big for them and they feel out of their depth – then they're being honest. Nobody needs advice from people who don't know what they're talking about. In this instance, good friends would look for outside help. They may approach the school counsellor, a GP, a trusted adult or teacher to lend a hand.

Following are some all-too-common situations that many kids have to face. And without the help of good friends like you they could be facing the problem alone. After reading this section, you will know what to do should a good mate of yours find herself in one of these predicaments.

DIVORCE AND FAMILY BREAK-UPS – Couples fall out of love all the time, despite the promises they have made to each other and in spite of the fact that they have children.

The truth of the matter is that some couples live pretty big lies. They pretend to be happy and then one day it all gets too much and someone makes a decision to split. With such a big trauma set in motion it's hardly surprising that most kids with divorcing parents are left feeling alone, frightened and very confused.

> *"Marie and I had been close friends for years. She was one of the nicest people I knew, but overnight she changed. She suddenly became sulky and would often be mean and spiteful for no reason. We fought all the time. Then one night when I was ready to give up on her, she came round and spilled it all out. Her parents were divorcing and she was being made to go and live with her mum. It was terrible and she cried and cried. After that things were better between us and I was more understanding."*
> Karen, 15

At this very moment there are over two hundred thousand children in the UK involved in their parents' divorce proceedings. Statistics also show that over fifty per cent of divorced parents remarry. This means that tens of thousands of step-families will come into being. To adjust to such enormous changes in their life, your friend will need all the non-judgemental support that you can offer.

How to help

1 Try to understand what your friend is going through. She may believe that she no longer has a 'real' family and that her parents don't love her. And deep, deep down she may be hoping that this nightmare will pass and that her parents will get back together again. Your friend might be pretending that none of this bothers her when inside she's secretly crying.

2 Accept that you can't be a fairy godmother and make everything OK; you can only listen and comfort her. Tell her that she has every right to be angry, to cry and to scream. No one expects her to be happy or good tempered about this dire situation. If she feels depressed, get her to talk about all the things that are worrying her. Reassure her that other people are equally concerned and would also be happy to listen and talk to her.

3 If you can get your friend to pin-point exactly the things that are making her unhappy, you may be able to help her in a more practical way. For instance, is she particularly upset by the fact that she will have to move away? If this is the problem, let her know that you will still be her friend no matter where she lives. Or is it the perpetual feuding between her parents that's getting her down? Is she unhappy because she thinks the truth is being kept from her?

4 Make sure your friend really believes that she is not at fault. She must understand that it's her parents who have the problem, not her.

5 Tell her that she doesn't have to take sides. Your friend must make decisions about the whole situation that are in her best interest. For example, she must not let one parent use her to gain information about the other.

6 If it's the thought of being in a step-family surrounded by step-siblings and a step-parent that's worrying her, tell her that even though it will be stressful and strange for a while she must give her new family a chance. Point out that she has nothing to lose and everything to gain by really trying to make a go of the whole thing.

FRIENDS WHO HATE THEIR FAMILIES – I remember visiting a friend whose family was constantly warring. Simple, everyday gripes became full-blown family confrontations. If someone borrowed something that belonged to another member of the family, my friend's family would be screaming and yelling abuse at each other within minutes. I know I had rows with my brothers, but they were nothing like the battles that raged every day in my friend's house.

Another of my friends disliked her brother so much that she cut up all his clothes and flushed them down the toilet. This is a pretty desperate act. If one of your friends 'hates' her family or lives with constant arguing and fighting, then she needs your help. She may also need somewhere to go to escape the pitched battle for a while.

*"My best friend hates her sister so much. She says
she is always being forced to baby-sit and has to share all
her stuff with her sister. I can't go round there without seeing
my friend in tears over something her sister has done. I agree
that her sister is annoying but I think my friend over-reacts.
My friend hits her sister and this then gets her into loads
of trouble with her parents. I hate to see my friend so
unhappy. I'd like to help but I don't know how."*

Susie, 14

Siblings (and parents, for that matter) are a law unto themselves. What may look like a family at war may be a family under stress. This doesn't mean that they don't really love each other, just that for some reason they are unable to express it. Chances are that if one member of the family was in trouble or was bad-mouthed, then the rest of the family would stand up for her or him. Families are funny things, so you must not judge the family of a friend hastily or thoughtlessly.

How to help

1 If your friend is always fighting with other members of her family, ask your friend if she thinks that her own behaviour may contribute to the trouble. Does she needlessly hassle her younger sister and then go totally ballistic when the sister seeks some kind of revenge? Does your friend leave her stuff all over the house and then lose her rag when she finds that someone has borrowed her belongings? Does she have an all-in brawl with her parents every time they refuse to let her go out? Maybe all your friend has to do to put an end to the fighting is change her behaviour. If she stopped annoying her sister, kept her things stored away and spoke sensibly to her parents rather than throwing a wobbly, then things at home might be different.

2 If a friend thinks one of her siblings hates her, try and get her to talk to her brother or sister. She should ask them why they're so mean all the time. They may not even realise just how awful they are being. All it takes to rectify such a situation is for someone to say something.

3 Sometimes people just don't get on with their parents. Issues like privacy, independence, values and morals often get in the way of having a happy relationship with parents. If nothing your friend does is ever right in her parents' eyes or vice versa, then all you can do is listen. It may help to let her know that you too have similar problems with your parents. Let's face it – everybody feels at certain times that their parents are the worst in the world.

4 If your friend says she hates her family, try to find out if there is a serious problem. Is she being hurt by someone in her family? Is she in trouble and too afraid to ask for help? This sort of problem may need special help from trained and qualified counsellors.

For help and advice contact:
CHILDLINE
Freephone 0800 1111

FRIENDS WITH DRUG-DEPENDENT PARENTS – This is a tough one. Your friend will be afraid but may pretend that she can tough it out. Your friend might also blame herself and even be ashamed of her parents. What you as a good friend have to do is urge her to get help and to get it quickly. She has to accept that she can't stop her parents from either drinking or using drugs, that she is not at fault and that she can't cope alone. No amount of pleading by your friend will make her parents' dependency go away. She is also risking her own life at the same time. Drug dependencies cause erratic behaviour – her parents may become violent and unleash their fury on your friend.

"My friend is having such a tough time right now. Her mum is a drinker and because of this my friend has to do everything around the house. She has to look after her younger brother, cook and look after her mum. Her mum is so mean when she drinks, she swears and tells my friend her drinking is her fault.

Once she didn't come home for two days and my friend was out of her mind with worry. I am the only one who knows about this and I'm not much help to her."
Sophie, 15

How to help

1 Point out to your friend that covering up for her parents when they either drink or abuse other drugs achieves nothing. If anything, concealing the problem makes it easier for her parents to continue their drinking or drug-taking. Your friend mustn't rush round clearing up for them and mustn't get involved in buying alcohol or other drugs for them. And above all your friend mustn't let her parents' problem cause her further problems. For example, skiving off school to look after an unwell parent or not doing homework because she has to do the shopping. Hard as it will be for your friend, she must not make excuses for her parents' behaviour.

2 Your friend needs you to listen and to listen without being judgemental. If you are saying nasty things about her parents then your friend will clam-up – she won't tell you the full story. She may even start to lie about the situation at home.

3 Sometimes being a good friend means seeking help on her behalf. If you're frightened that your friend's health and welfare are in danger, then tell a trusted adult. Your friend may have asked you to keep everything she's told you secret, but some secrets just aren't meant to be kept.

For information and counselling contact:
ALATEEN
61 Great Dover Street, London SE1 4YF.
Tel: 0171 403 0888.

THE NATIONAL DRUGS HELPLINE
Freephone 0800 77 66 00

FRIENDS WITH EATING DISORDERS – It is usually a friend who first recognises that a mate has an eating disorder. Why? Because a pal notices even the smallest changes in their friend's attitude, dress and behaviour. Your friend wears a new pair of earring studs – you notice. Your friend does her hair differently – you notice. Your friend doesn't join in when you go for a burger or they behave oddly after eating – you notice. Friends can see things that parents can't.

Anorexics will lie about their eating habits, starve themselves and exercise rigorously, while bulimics will binge eat. This means that they will eat until they make themselves vomit or they will induce vomiting. Both anorexia and bulimia are life-threatening and if you suspect that a friend has one of these eating disorders you must act quickly.

*"My friend went on a diet a few months back.
Since then she has lost loads of weight and become
very thin. But I worry about her because she is always
lying about her eating habits. She says she eats her lunch but
I know she doesn't. She has fainted twice recently and I think
it has something to do with this crazy diet she is on. Also
she is acting really strangely; she is moody, withdrawn
and she is always tired. Her skin is the most awful
colour and her hair is all lank and dull. Thing is,
if I say something to her or to her parents
I know she is going to hate me."*
Julie, 16

How to help

1 Even though your friend will lash out when she finds that you have sought help for her, you have to believe that you have done the right thing. In time, your friend will thank you for everything you did.

2 Anorexia and bulimia are not about dieting or wanting to be skinny, they are serious illnesses. A sufferer can literally starve herself to death. This is why you have to seek help so that your friend can receive the professional help she needs.

3 Don't try to force your friend to eat, it won't work and in fact may make things worse. Your friend's problem stems from a lack of self-esteem and a feeling of being powerless, and these won't be solved by simply making her eat three square meals.

4 Respect your friend's privacy by not blabbing to all and sundry.

The Eating Disorders Association
Sackville Place, 44 Magdalen Street,
Norwich, Norfolk NR3 1JE.
Tel: 0603 621414

FRIENDS WHO ARE BEING ABUSED – When we think of abuse, we usually think about sexual abuse but this is just one type of abuse.

There is also physical abuse where someone hits or shoves another person. Then there's verbal abuse when a person is being constantly shouted at and being called offensive and humiliating names. Verbal abuse destroys someone's self-confidence and self-esteem. Neglect is another form of abuse. This occurs when a person, most usually a child, is not being cared for properly. The child may be left alone for long periods, she may not be fed or she may be forced to live in conditions that are detrimental to her health and well-being.

The remaining form of abuse is self-inflicted abuse. This means that a person does deliberate physical damage to themselves. She does this because she feels worthless or as a way of punishing herself.

If you have a friend who is being abused or is self-abusing, you have to encourage her to seek help immediately. If she won't, then you will have to seek help on her behalf.

" I'm worried about a friend of mine. I think she is being hit by her boyfriend. Every time I try to speak to her about it she denies it, but I've seen the bruises and I've seen him when he's angry."
Anne, 16

How to help

1 Make sure your friend understands that she is not to blame for what is happening. Abusers often get away with their behaviour by manipulating the victim into thinking that everything is her fault. They also threaten the victim so that she is too scared to tell anyone what is going on. Your friend has to accept that there is no excuse for someone sexually molesting her, hitting her or shouting abuse at her.

2 If you have a friend who is injuring herself, it can be pretty frightening. But what you don't do is physically try to stop her; it won't make things better. Best thing to do is listen to her and encourage her to seek professional help.

Childline
Freephone 0800 1111

The Bristol Crisis Service For Women
PO Box 654,
Bristol BS99 1XH,
This agency specialises in helping women who want to inflict physical damage on themselves. Counsellors will also offer advice to those wanting to help friends and family members.

FRIENDS WHO HAVE BEEN BEREAVED – Seeing a friend you care about lose a parent, sibling or other close relative is one of the hardest things to cope with. You may be unsure about what you can and should do. You will be frightened of saying and doing the wrong thing and upsetting your friend even more. Is it best to leave her alone to grieve or is it best to be with her? Will people think you're a bit morbid if you go to visit her? These feelings of helplessness, fear and worry often make you decide to stay away until your friend makes contact with you. But part and parcel of being a good friend is being with her even during the most painful times.

Your presence might be just what your friend needs. Maybe she can open up to you about her feelings in a way that she can't with her family. She too may be frightened of saying the wrong thing to her family.

"When my mum died it was terrible, hardly any of my friends came round and the ones who did couldn't even look me in the face. For weeks afterwards I'd spot school friends crossing the road to avoid me – it was really hurtful. Even now, friends act weird towards me if I talk about my mum. I get the impression that they think I should be over her death by now, or that I shouldn't make them feel bad by talking about her."
Emma, 15

How to help

1 Don't frighten yourself by thinking you have to do something to ease your friend's pain. There is nothing you can do but be there and listen.

2 Don't be surprised if your friend doesn't cry at first. Shock and denial are natural responses to death.

3 Be aware that there is no time limit to grief.

4 Don't avoid bringing up the subject of death or the person who has died. If your friend feels that you are embarrassed or feel awkward, then she will stop talking to you about her feelings.

5 Don't be afraid to admit to others that the whole process of death and dying scares you.

6 If you really can't face your friend or even talk to her on the phone, then write a letter. This will show that you are thinking of her.

CHAPTER **nine**

Friends for life

Not all of your friends will be friends for life. Over the years some will drift away without you even noticing, while others will be very sad partings. Sometimes friendships will unfortunately end with a bang – nasty circumstances making it impossible for the friendship to continue. But then – and this is the good bit – there will be friends who will stick around to see you finish college, will wave goodbye at the airport when you go on your travels, and will help you out when love-type relationships go off the rails. These guys will be still hanging around when you're celebrating your 60th birthday.

The fact is, you just never know how long or short a friendship will be, which is why you should always try make the most of all your friendships.

> *"Some of my best friendships have only lasted a couple of years. But I still think about these friends. I don't think we'd have much in common now, but we certainly did back then."*
> Claire, 18

You may disagree with the above. You may believe that you can make friendships last – and you might be right. If you and your friends are willing and happy to put in the effort for the long haul then it will most

probably pay off. But everyone involved must be flexible and accommodating. You may all have to let go of some old promises and dreams. What seemed possible a year ago in your friendship may be impossible when you're both studying at different colleges, working in different sorts of jobs, or have families. Friendships change and grow just like people.

I've known my oldest friend for twenty-five years. When we were seven we were neighbours and the best of friends. Our bedroom windows faced each other and at night we'd communicate via flashing torches. During the long summer holidays we'd make promises to share a flat when we were older, and assured each other that we'd only go out with men who were best friends too.

When we got older, went to different schools, emerged with different interests and at one stage lived at different ends of the country, we communicated only by the occasional letter. But the friendship survived. It survived because we both accepted the fact that we're no longer best friends. We no longer discuss the day-to-day stuff like I do with my current best friends, but we do laugh about what we used to do and giggle about the promises we once made. It is no longer a best-friend relationship, but it is still a friendship that we both treasure.

Time isn't important

I also have a very close friend whom I've only known for a short period. We don't yet have a history together but I can honestly say, with hand on heart, that she knows me better than anyone else. For when it comes to real friendship, time is rarely a factor. It can play as big or as little a role as you want it to. Some friends you'll know for five minutes and feel like you've known them for years, others you'll have known for years before you decide that you want to be friends.

> *"Cathy and I have been in the same class since junior school. We always got on but were never what you'd call friends. Then three years ago I bumped into her on the way home from school and we just talked and talked. Almost overnight we became best friends."*
> Amy, 16

> *"I met Caroline in the strangest way. She was my boyfriend's ex-girlfriend and when I met her at a party, we hit it off immediately. I mean, it could have been awful but it wasn't. Even after I split up with my boyfriend, we hung out together. Caroline and I can hardly remember him now, but we're grateful to him because he brought us together."*
> Yvonne, 18

Growing apart

The sad part of any friendship is when you both decide that you no longer want to be friends. If you're lucky it will be decided mutually and it will happen without any fuss or bother. If you're unlucky it will be a big painful scene with lots of tears. Friendship is a two-way thing – it's a partnership – and if one person no longer wants to participate in the friendship then there's nothing that can be done to reverse the situation.

Tell-tale signs of a friendship gone wrong

BEING COPIED – This is the most annoying thing in the world. It makes you angry because you have no control over what's happening.

Being copied isn't a compliment. It's a sign that something's not right within a friendship. Maybe the boundaries between the two of you have become blurred or your friend is trying to find herself through you. The best way to deal with it is to talk about it. If your friend refuses to or denies there is a problem, you'll have to keep your distance for a while.

"I knew Mari had always liked the way I dressed but it never bothered me until we both started dating. Then she'd do things like turn up in a similar outfit to me. She'd wear the same jewellery, take on my mannerisms and even say she fancied the boys that I fancied. The last straw was when she had her hair cut and coloured like me. I told her that I didn't want to see her any more. My mum said I was being unnecessarily harsh because being copied is a big compliment. But it didn't feel like a compliment, it felt like she was trying to be me."
June, 16

BEING TAKEN FOR GRANTED – This is a sign that a friendship is out of balance, and one partner is either giving or taking far more than the other. If you don't have a fair relationship where both friends make the effort to get together, talk on the phone or arrange outings, then one partner is always going to be upset with the other.

Sometimes a friend will accidentally take a mate for granted. They don't realise that their behaviour is unreasonable. What's the solution? Have a talk about it and do it now before bitterness and resentment rear their ugly heads.

"Kerry does things like call me up at the last minute and cancel stuff. One time, she called me half an hour after she was supposed to come round, to say that she didn't feel like going out. When we do go out, she always wants everything her way, and if I say no, she threatens to go home. It never used to be like this and I don't know how to put our friendship right again."
Linda, 15

Sometimes, however, the inconsiderate behaviour is very deliberate. It is intended as a very crude and immature way of saying the friendship is over. Instead of telling her friend that it is time to part company, she takes this sneaky way out. If you feel that a friend is trying to give you the heavy-handed hint, your best bet is to confront her about it. Ask her what the problem is (though sometimes there isn't a problem) and then decide together whether the friendship is worth saving.

BICKERING – Arguing, bitching and sniping at each other are all signs that something is up. There are, of course, some friendships where most of the communication is carried on in this nasty way, but these sorts of friendships are the exception. On the whole, most healthy relationships are based on cool, calm and reasoned conversation. If your friendship has dissolved into a verbal slanging match, it's time to call it a day.

> *"We argue all the time about the silliest things. Even simple chit-chat is impossible because both of us seem to be taking everything the wrong way. It's got to the stage where we can't even apologise without arguing."*
> Tina, 15

If you want to save your friendship there are two things you can both do. One, stop being defensive. When people are insecure or anxious about something they will often go ape at even the most harmless and innocent comments. This is because they imagine that there is some hidden barb in what was said. This in turn makes the person who has made the comment go on the offensive and the fighting starts all over again.

Two, start listening instead of talking. Perhaps your friend has a point to what she's saying, maybe she wants to make up too. Or then again, she may be trying to say that the friendship's over.

BEING AFRAID TO SAY SOMETHING – There is no difference between this and being afraid to be honest with each other. Where there is no honesty, there is no friendship – period.

> *"Sophie gets on my nerves and I want to tell her that she's not as cool as she thinks she is, but I'm afraid to. She has a terrible temper and gets mad whenever someone tries to tell her something. I don't want Sophie to turn on me."*
> Helen, 15

"I know Karen's boyfriend is having an affair but I can't bring myself to tell Karen. I'm worried that she won't believe me or that she'll hate me for telling her."
Liz, 15

If a friend throws a wobbly when you try to reason or be honest with her, then you've both got a problem. She can't accept a bit of well-intentioned advice from a friend, and you're stuck in a bit of a tricky spot. By not being honest or by not being able to be honest, you're cheating the friendship. Underneath your 'good friend' intentions, you're really more worried about yourself. For example, you're frightened of being shouted at, being made to feel guilty or being put into a position where you lose face with your friend.

The only way out is to be totally up front by accepting that you have to do what's best for your friend whatever the consequences. So take a deep breath and go for it.

Short-term friends

Not all friendships can stand the test of time. Some are destined to last for years and years, while others are only good for a few months. This doesn't mean that short-term friendships are less valuable than long-term ones. All it means is that they are different.

"Sue and I broke up with our boyfriends at the same time, so we spent lots of time crying and talking about what went wrong in our relationships. Then, after a few months I started to feel better while she remained depressed. I suddenly realised that the only thing we had in common was our broken relationships."
Lisa, 14

"We used to be such great friends, but these days she's too busy with her athletics to see me. All she does is go on about how I should get fit and stop eating chocolate. Anything to do with my life simply doesn't interest her."
Tracey, 16

Friendships like Lisa's and Sue's occur when two people have similar problems and need each other. Unfortunately, once the original problem has been resolved there is often not much left upon which to build a friendship.

Sometimes, as Tracey discovered, friendships end because other things become more important. As sad as it is to lose a friend, it's important not to hold on. Instead, let go and see what happens. Perhaps your friend will drift away or maybe she'll stick around and become a different kind of friend. Maybe she'll wise up and make the effort to be a proper friend again. Unless you loosen your grip, you'll never know.

The rough patches

Rocky periods in a friendship are common. How many times have you thought 'I've had just about enough of you, I'm off'? And how many times have you said to yourself 'Mmm ... maybe I was being a bit mean, perhaps I should give her a call'? If you're like most peeps you've probably done both of these things more often than you care to remember. I know I have. In a friendship you have to learn to take the good with the bad, the high times with the low times. If you can cope with the rough spots, your friendships will be strengthened.

Survival tips

1 In any friendship there will be times when one partner will need lots of help, support, tolerance and patience from the other. A healthy friendship has room for these and as long as the friend works her way through her problems, your friendship will survive.

2 Sometimes a friend will make a decision that you think is really bad for her. Maybe she's decided to go back to her cheating boyfriend or to drop out of school. To survive these trying times, you have to learn that you don't control your friend's life. You can say your piece and tell her how you feel, but you can only hope that she'll take your advice. If she doesn't, then accept her decision.

3 There is no getting away from the fact that people change. If a friend has changed, either physically or mentally (but not in a nasty way), you may feel that she is not the person you once liked. But what you've got to do is look beyond the new 'wrapping'. Allowing your friends to change is like saying, 'It's OK to be whoever you want'. Isn't that what you would like to hear from a friend if you had undergone some changes?

4 Surviving the rough patches also means knowing when to pull out. You have to know when enough is enough. If a friendship is causing you untold problems, then your survival as a happy, healthy person will depend on you ending the relationship.

Losing a friend

"Two years ago my best friend died in a car accident. I can't believe how much I miss her. I don't know what to do."
Rebecca, 17

Losing a friend you love is never easy to come to terms with. The only way to deal with it is to take one day at a time and to realise that death is an inevitable part of all our lives.

When a friend dies it suddenly brings home the fact that you and your other friends are not invincible. It could just as easily have been yourself or someone else who had died. But it's useless to worry about death because the worrying will stop you from enjoying the present. Don't let your fears take over your life and ruin the memory of your friend.

Anyone who suffers a bereavement has to grieve. Grieving is not just for relatives. When you grieve there are distinct stages: shock, anger, denial, depression and finally acceptance.

If there is no family member who can help you through this period, then seek the advice of a bereavement counsellor. A counsellor will reassure you, among many other things, that you should not feel guilty for getting on with your life when the time is right. Going out, having a good time and making other friends does not mean that you have forgotten your deceased friend or were not a true friend.

"I became an artist because of a friend who was in my art class. When we were 14 she said that one day my paintings would hang in a museum. She died before that happened but she's on my mind every time I start a new painting."
Shanna, 24

Friends for life

You can get by without lots of things, but your life is much the poorer without friends. After all, good friends teach you to like yourself by showing you all your good points. Sometimes they even show you how to like yourself despite your bad ones.

I did a quick straw poll among my friends and the guys in the office to find out what makes good friendships and what makes them last. Some of the people I spoke to were in their teens, others were in their late forties, but despite these differences their ideas about friendship were surprisingly similar. The following five points were mentioned by everyone I spoke to.

TREASURE YOUR TIME TOGETHER – Going out with a friend and having a terrifically exciting time is great, but the most rewarding aspect of a friendship is doing the day-to-day junk together. You know the kind of stuff: watching TV and bingeing out on chocolates, discussing the latest crush, listening to the radio, painting each other's fingernails, and spending a whole day trying on each other's clothes. Even just hanging out and watching the rest of the world go by is extra special when done with a friend.

BE INDEPENDENT – Just because you're friends doesn't mean you have to live in each other's pocket and do everything together. If you both develop separate interests and have other friends it will mean that your relationship will never get stuck in a rut. Whenever you see each other, you'll both have new things to talk about and share.

LAUGH HEAPS – Being crazy together can haul a friendship through many a bad time. Life is sometimes pretty rotten and the only sure-fire remedy is a mega bout of laughing with a good friend. In fact, being able to share a good giggle is often the main reason for two people getting together in the first place.

BEING A GOOD LISTENER – Good friends are good listeners. This does not mean that one partner can run off at the mouth while the other stays mute. There are, of course, times in every relationship when someone has to be willing to listen while the other offloads their worries.

SHARING – This is more than just letting your friend borrow your fave jumper, it means being willing to share the troublesome parts of each other's life. By revealing your worries and concerns to a friend, you are giving that friend a chance to show how much they care. So, go on and let a friend show you what they're made of.

FACING THE FUTURE – A relationship that survives by remembering and harking back to the 'good old days' is not as strong as one that keeps moving forward and creating new memories every day. One relationship could be said to be in a rut; the other, vibrant and alive. The only way to have a living friendship is to actively go for it. Take your friendship for granted and it may become just a memory.

The nitty-gritty about the best books around

Am I Normal?
Just Seventeen's agony aunt, Anita Naik gives down-to-earth answers to all those awkward questions that keep you awake at night.

Families: can't live with them, can't live without them!
No one gets on with their nearest and dearest all the time – but, with help from Anita Naik, learning to live together may be easier than you think!

Is This Love?
From flirting and first dates to jealousy and break-ups, Anita Naik helps you to handle all the ups and downs of love.

The Just Seventeen Guide to being Gorgeous
Want to know how to make the most of what you've got? Adele Lovell gives you the low-down on hair, skin, make-up, healthy eating and much more.

Stand up for Yourself!
Helen Benedict's book explains how to handle all kinds of problems which may crop up on the street or in the home. Essential reading for all young people who want to protect themselves without getting paranoid.

Don't just sit there – Get A Life!
Ever feel you're in a rut? Think you should be having more fun? Do you panic when someone suggests 'doing something exciting'? If you answered 'yes' to these questions, you need this book! Victoria McCarthy shows how you can take control of your life and change it for the better.

Everything you ever wanted to know about periods ... but didn't like to ask!
Charlotte Owen's essential book explains all you'll ever need to know about one of the most important times in your life! Recommended by Brook Advisory Centres

Life, Love and High Marks
Homework, tests, more homework, exams – how can you possibly
have a life? Kate Brookes gives you the essential tips on how to plan your time
at school and at home so that you get the best of work and play!

Respect Yourself
Low on self-esteem? Need to build your self-confidence? Anita Naik
teaches you how to be your own best friend.

Body Talk
Wondering how to get the object of your desire to notice
you? Want to ask mum to do a small (well, huge, actually) favour?
With Victoria McCarthy's help, you'll be able to make
the most of your bodytalk.

Torn in Two
Matthew Whyman's refreshing and sensitive books offers
reassurance and guidance on dealing with your parents' divorce, right
from the moment you suspect that there's trouble in store.

Keep Your Options Open
Choosing your options at school? Deciding whether to stay
on in education or to get a job? Read Vivienne Neale's essential
guide to making the choices that are right for you.